WE'RE NOT DONE YET, POP

Published by Lisa Hagan Books 2018

www.lisahaganbooks.com

We're Not Done Yet, Pop:

My Lessons from the Other Side

Joe McQuillen

Helping Parents Heal has been grateful to invite Joe McQuillen to speak at several of our meetings over the past few years. He is one of our favorite presenters and entertains our parents with stories of his deep connection with Christopher.

Joe would seem to be an unlikely candidate to pursue spiritual enlightenment. He grew up in a blue-collar neighborhood outside of Buffalo, NY. Although Joe came from a strong Irish Catholic background he thought little about the afterlife or the possibility of connecting with his son Christopher before he passed. However, Christopher was very insistent. Through his son, Joe has written two remarkable books based on his channeled writing from Christopher.

Joe McQuillen's newest book, entitled 'We're Not Done Yet, Pop' follows his first, 'My Search for Christopher on the Other Side.' In this book, Chris communicates with his dad through beautifully worded, almost other-worldly, messages that inspire Joe to move forward on his healing journey. This, in turn, helps other parents to know that their kids are not gone.

Joe describes several bittersweet moments throughout the book, such as a series of 'firsts' in his life since Christopher passed. Joe uses a markedly eloquent term borrowed from his wife, Sally: *brutiful*, meaning a beautiful and brutal situation. This term, which may someday become a part of our vernacular, evokes the quintessential feelings which accompany grief.

Channeling Christopher is not the only way that Joe communicates. He has tried many wonderful healing modalities that are described throughout the book. These can be as simple as a paper lantern launch or lighting a candle in honor of Christopher. Or can be as involved as meditation, Spirit Circles, Near Death Experiences, consulting Mediums, developing Clair Senses, Exit Points and Soul Contracts, learning about Heaven, Spirit and Animal Guides, and Astral Travel.

Joe's book is an easy-to-follow guide to finding out what best connects each of us with our loved ones in spirit. Throughout the book, Joe and Christopher offer evidence that our kids are still right here, sharing in every significant event and helping us move forward and heal.

As Joe so beautifully writes: "Just follow the breadcrumbs, and you will be ok. Trust me on this. Whether you are trying to find your own spiritual path or just making it through the day, rely on spirit and follow the signs."

I highly recommend Joe McQuillen's book. It is written by a professed ordinary guy who has undertaken an extraordinary journey to find his son in spirit and thus lead a joyful, purpose-filled life. He is proof that spirit communication is available to all of us. And the reader cannot help falling in love with them both.

-Elizabeth Boisson
President and Co-Founder, *Helping Parents Heal, Inc*
www.helpingparentsheal.org

CONTENTS

On January 3, 2016, my son, Christopher and three of his friends drowned in a canoe accident on Lake Beulah, Wisconsin. The boys were all in their early twenties. As Christmas vacation was coming to a close, a dozen or so friends met at the lake house of one of their parents. It was supposed to be a last hurrah before school started up again that winter. At around three o'clock in the morning, the four pals walked past a boathouse and decided to take a three-man canoe out in a partially frozen lake. None of them made it back. This book is a follow-up to *My Search for Christopher on the Other Side*, which chronicled my search and connection with my boy, during the first two years after his crossing over. What I discovered has changed my path, and it's changed my life. *"Life isn't about waiting for the storm to pass...It's about learning to dance in the rain,"* wrote Vivian Greene. Please share this dance with me... with us.

CHAPTER ONE:

WE'RE NOT DONE YET

On August 5, 2018, I returned home to Illinois from a week-long annual family reunion in Crystal Beach, Ontario. Only a few days earlier was the thirty-first-month anniversary—January 3, 2016—of my son Christopher's drowning and subsequent crossing over to the other side. It was a lifetime ago, and it was yesterday. I'm stealing a phrase used by my wife Sally when I say the Canada trip was brutiful. It was beautiful, as it was a chance to immerse myself and my family in all things McQuillen—love, support, sarcasm, humor, fierce loyalty, and as most things Irish, a sense of tradition. And it was brutal because every other turn took me back to a time when my Christopher ran through the little enclave with reckless abandon. Like most Irish families, if you scratch the surface you will find at its heart one of a poet. However, the execution is not always flawless. I so badly wanted to launch a Chinese lantern from the sands of Crystal Beach, Ontario. However, Sally and the kids left for home a day or two earlier than I did, and Sally repacked the lanterns and brought them back to Illinois.

Upon my arrival home, I waited until dusk, grabbed my Labrador Cassidy, and headed to Chris's grave to launch the lantern. I carried my ditty bag with gravestone cleaning and trimming accoutrements, my Buffalo Bills folding chair, and a collapsed Chinese lantern with a waxed candle block included.

See lantern-launching instructions below.

STEPS

1. Choose a safe launch site. In the vast majority of cases, sky lanterns are perfectly safe and fun.
2. Launch during good weather.
3. Open your lantern.
4. Fill your lantern with air.
5. Light the fuel source.
6. Let go and enjoy!
7. Make a wish (optional).

Looks easy, doesn't it? We've launched lanterns in the past and it's always a bit tricky. Last night, I unwrapped my lantern, attached the wax block candle, and lit it. I laid it on the ground for the candle to inflate the paper lantern and... the grass on which the lantern sat was dry and it caught fire! The spreading grassfire then set the paper lantern ablaze. Cassidy began barking at, and feigning an attack on, the blazing lantern wilting now on the spreading prairie grassfire. So much for perfectly executed tradition. But it was funnier than hell and I know my boy Chris was laughing and encouraging likeminded spirits to enjoy the shit show his dad and dog were putting on at his grave. After extinguishing the fire, discarding all incriminating evidence, and a quick apology for the now-singed grave to its occupant, I pulled up my chair next to Chris's grave, lit a cigar, and began to tell my son about the previous week in Canada.

Arriving in Canada after a nine-hour drive is always tricky. I like to hit Wegmans (the greatest supermarket in the world) while passing through Buffalo to stock up on Sahlen's hot dogs, soda, beer, buns, condiments, and cereal, and then head to the border.

Halfway along the Peace Bridge we cross from U.S. to Canadian soil; American flags on one side of a white line, Canadian flags right next to it on the other. Below us the mighty Niagara River is flowing toward the falls.

The kids, even as young adults, would sit up at this point and take it all in. It reminds me of being a kid, and being a dad, and now of losing a son. See, that's what happens. That's how it goes. One moment you're enjoying the view of the river below, and the next, you're stumbling on a memory chest-deep in grief.

This no longer surprises me. I have learned to let the current of grief take me until I can again find my footing. Terra firma, my solid ground.

Back at his grave, Chris and I have our talk under the stars. It's quiet of course and surrounded by woods so I take the heavy summer air into my lungs, while looking up at the stars in the western sky. It's mostly me processing, as he was there with us in Canada. But I run down the previous week's events, especially that last night on Friday, August 3. Sally and the kids had headed home the day before. (The third of the month is always melancholy for me as my boy left this world on the third of January 2016.) I had exited the nightly family celebration a little early as I usually do. It involved a cookout, lots of cocktails (none for me of course), and a rousing stint of Karaoke. Kids, teens, young adults, and the old guard, all taking their turn with surprisingly little prompting and tumultuous applause at the end regardless of the quality of the performance.

I slipped away with no goodbyes, as usual, and headed to our rented beach house walking the small streets of Crystal Beach, Ontario that my Chris had walked the first week of August for the better part of a decade. I arrived, to a now-empty house, feeling restless. So, I grabbed a cigar and headed to the beach. The moon was clear, the lake was calm. There were a few pockets of families ending their summer evening with a small fire or walking ankle deep in the surf, but mostly I was alone. Or maybe not. I almost always connect with Chris on beaches at night. (I experienced my strongest connection with Chris on a beach at night in Sarasota, Florida in 2016.) But it's rare that I don't feel him around me on any beach at night. Maybe it's because when I walk on the beach my intention is to connect. Even before my feet hit the sand, I reach out to him through the field to let him know I'm heading to a beach to talk. As sure as I'm writing this, I feel a tingle on the back of my neck and an energy wash over me. My Chris is present, and we are connected.

If you haven't read *My Search for Christopher on the Other Side* yet, put this book down and get it. A lot of what I discuss going forward will only make sense once you've read and embraced what's in that book.

In *My Search…*, I chronicled the first two years after my son crossed over; this book picks up where the first one left off. The visits with Chris continue as does my search, through private readings, as well as public appearances by authors, healers, and mediums—anyone and anything that deals with the other side. Anything metaphysical. The metaphysical is defined as transcending physical matter or the laws of nature. Merriam-Webster defines metaphysical as: *"of or relating to the transcendent or to a reality beyond what is perceptible to the senses."* If you're so inclined, you may read more on metaphysics in the Appendix at the back of this book.

The research I've done over the last five-plus years has taught me that we are spiritual beings—spiritual beings having a physical experience. So, what I thought was an original deduction wasn't. Maybe Pierre Teilhard de Chardin (May 1, 1881 – 10 April 10, 1955) said it best: *"We are not human beings having a spiritual experience; we are spiritual beings having a human experience."* Chardin was a philosopher and Jesuit priest who trained as a paleontologist and geologist. He was a scientist and a teacher. In 1925, however, Chardin fell out of favor with the Catholic Church for his teachings. As a result, none of this is new. Today, it's all just more widely accepted.

I also take exception to Merriam-Webster's definition of *"a reality beyond what is perceptible to the senses."* Because it is often my senses that tell me Chris's spirit is near. As I said earlier, I can feel his presence as a tingle on the back of my neck and all around me. When sitting in my office, oftentimes I can smell him—*that* smell of him. But then again, I'm a believer. It's not hard for me to buy in. In fact, I would be lost if I hadn't bought in—body, mind, and soul.

Chris had pushed me to finish the first book. And I thought I was done, that I had one story to tell, one truth to bring out. Boy, I was wrong. My son guided me through my first book and in the process, his prompting often bordered on harassment. A loving insistence to finish. But that was and is my son, Chris.

When the manuscript was finished just before Father's Day in 2018, as Chris requested, I had no idea what to do with it. I know lots of people and have lots of contacts but none in the world of metaphysical publishing. I did meet with a number of published authors; one who wrote spy novels, one who wrote books on business, and one who wrote a really heartfelt book about a final family trip with his aging parents and loving children. I also did a reading with a well-respected author and psychic who was going to put a word in for me with her publisher. But this approach was too passive for me and Chris. We wrote a book. We needed to get things rolling.

I've been told there are two routes to being published: self-publishing or getting a contract with a publishing house. With self-publishing, search Google and you'll find Amazon and others can handle it and they often print on demand, according to the number of orders. The good news is that you get to keep virtually all the proceeds. The bad news is how the hell does anyone outside of your friends (the ones who don't think you are completely off the reservation) and family (the ones who don't think you are completely off the reservation) know about it? Infomercials… I just couldn't see myself hawking this book on a commercial following the guy who saws a boat in half and glues it together. I was also told that once you self-publish you are dead to major publishers. Jeez, that seems a bit harsh.

Securing a contract with a publishing house is the second route. What I did learn from my *coffee with authors tour* was that this route requires a guide. The writer's version of Sacajawea (I had to Google the spelling). The writer I referred to earlier told me not only is a literary agent a must, but the agent has to be in the same field as the book's subject. He told me he wrote a book about taking an RV trip across the country with three generations of family knowing it would be his parents' last trip. The book is *The Ride of Our Lives: Roadside Lessons of an American Family,* by Mike Leonard. It's a fabulous book. You should pick it up. Although the book is about a family journey he ended up at a book signing at a Bass Pro Shop and RV Center. Someone missed the point.

Armed with this valuable piece of info on publishing—self vs. publishing house—and a few too many extra-shot iced lattes, I returned home to scan the internet. I narrowed my search to publishers and agents who have dealt with the subject of the afterlife. I sent out a few emails with a description of my book. I found one agent who was also a publisher. Wow, two for one! Her name was Lisa Hagan and her reviews were outstanding. I looked deeper and saw some *New York Times* bestselling authors in her stable. My eyes kept going back to her name. For some reason, I didn't just send Lisa the description or a biography.

I sent her my book, which I subsequently learned is actually a manuscript. Lisa got back to me a few days later and said she read the first few chapters and was surprised that with the subject being what it was, it still made her laugh. She discussed the book over lunch with her mom. Hey, if she hangs out with her mom, she is *my kind of gal*. She then told me she was quite busy and that she would get back to me later in the summer. In my first book, I described what time was to an A.D.D. kid (or adult) per an expert on the subject. "There are two kinds of time," he said. "Now... and not now." Well, later in the summer fit squarely in the category of *NOT NOW*. Lisa did mention that while reading the book she felt Chris's presence...so I had that going for me.

A few weeks later, I was working from home attempting to will a response from Lisa, when an idea hit. I can't just email back to her and say, "What? Well, how about now?" But I did get the notion that everybody likes chocolate, and my dear pal Rick Blommer as in the Blommer Chocolate Family, had just dropped off some amazing gift boxes of chocolate that I spread around to lawyers and realtors in my other job... so why not? I emailed Lisa and asked if she wanted a box of premium chocolate. Even if she didn't want any at least it would open a dialogue, right? Well, she emailed back that she loved chocolate and had just run out of Swiss Chocolate (her fave) and would welcome a box of chocolate. Not long after I sent the chocolate, she emailed me back that she received it and that she also finished the book and wanted to work with me on it. This may seem like a coincidence to you. And maybe a few years ago I would have felt the same. But now I know that a coincidence is merely *God showing off*. Chris pushed me to write the book and guided me to an agent who gets it.

As I write this, I look down at a picture of my boy on the bottom of the computer screen smiling this sideways smile that is so frigging disarming, so charming and so sweet. And I know it was all his doing. The choice of agent, her mom, the chocolate—all of it. It was pure Chris in action. Pure Chris in spirit. I know in my heart that you have a Chris in your life, on the other side, who you need to connect with. To talk to and be guided by. So, open up your mind (I would say third eye but it's early in the book and I might lose you). Just hang in there.

The editing process was trying. It is difficult to have someone outside your circle critique and sometimes change what you have written.

Nonetheless, the edits arrived in spurts and I could see the wisdom in most of them; in others, I knew I needed to push back or stand my ground. After all, it's my story and Chris's story. Editing is a high-wire balancing act. We got through it.

Suffice it to say, the book got published. Lisa Hagan and her business partner Beth have their own publishing house. I had nightmares about selling my rights to a publisher that didn't fully get it, and what the subsequent result might look like. After receiving a few rejection letters from outside publishers, Lisa decided to pull any offers from remaining houses and do it herself. Lisa receives about 300 manuscript queries a week to review. But none of them come with the relentless Chris McQ delivery service. I shouldn't have been surprised. And I wasn't. It was in the stars from the beginning. I know that now. But at the time, waiting for anyone to publish the book was awful. How could a book that needs to be published possibly stall out? I couldn't even continue writing this book because it only makes sense on the heels of *My Search for Christopher*. So, when Lisa emailed me on the morning of October 10, 2018, that she wanted to publish our book through Lisa Hagan Books, I felt a rush of emotion. Relief, joy, and gratitude. Now, our book would be published by someone who gets it. Its integrity and beauty will remain intact.

Many fears can accompany writing a book. Any book. But the fear that a book is so precious to me and so necessary is heightened. I was afraid it wouldn't get published (it did), and I was afraid it would not be received well (it has). I was also afraid that my son Christopher, who was so instrumental in writing *My Search for Christopher on the Other Side*, may move on to other projects. Was it too much to hope my quickly evolving son would continue mentoring his spiritual slug of a dad, after the first book was published? Nope! He certainly has.

While writing *My Search*... I assumed it would be a one-and-done. We (Chris and I) had a story to tell. We told it. I was driven to get the story out. I knew that parents who have lost children needed someone to tell them they weren't really gone. Their kids were no more gone than Chris was. They are here. Their children's spirit is around them. Sure, it's a bad trade. Connecting with a child (or any loved one) on the other side is pure joy, love, and wonder. And I would trade all the connections I have had, all the awakenings, all the wonder for one walk on the beach. One ball game. But we don't have that option. We don't have a choice. Whatever event took our children from this life was a bell that cannot be un-rung.

During those first two years, I was exposed to so many amazing lessons. Connections, guided and unguided, signs and more signs. Feelings, facts, and miracles. Albert Einstein once said, "There are only two ways to live your life. One is as though nothing is a miracle. The other is as though everything is a miracle." This journey back and forth from a world I knew very little about prior to January 3, 2016 was overwhelming. Yet with all I have gathered and received, all I have reported, it dawned on me that I have only scratched the surface. I was a beginner, I needed to know more. You who are reading this and have lost someone dear, especially a child, deserve more. Buckle up.

It's just over three years since the book was published. The first year was a whirlwind of radio and internet interviews, with a few TV appearances and a handful of book signings in Chicago and Los Angeles (Book Soup) sprinkled in. Hollywood Baby— and of course, Buffalo, my hometown. I said yes to everything. I desperately wanted to get this book out there. I was scheduled to do a Skype interview with British filmmaker Kevin Moore a few months after the book was released. We were just discussing the story when he announced he decided to scrap the interview. He chose instead to shoot an in-person interview in the upcoming summer. He was coming to the U.S. to film a series of documentaries or a docuseries entitled, *They Call Us Channelers*. And that's exactly what he did. To date, he has published forty-six interviews, all on various forms of channeling, all things metaphysical. He showed up in Chicago and we shot the first half of the interview in my office, the room that used to be Chris's bedroom. We shot the second half of the interview at Chris's grave in Sacred Heart Cemetery. Chris's spirit moves freely in both spots, so it was appropriate to include both locations. I love that interview and was so very pleased that it was the first, in the series. As of today, our interview has had just over 73,000 views on YouTube. That's a lot of messages received. Chris and I are beyond grateful.

JANUARY 3, 2018

I guess it's time to go back to where I actually left off, after *My Search for Christopher on the Other side*. I ended the book on the second anniversary, January 3, 2018. Chris and I had our 3:00 a.m. visit chronicled in *My Search*... the group met at his grave at 3:30 p.m. Sally and I always secretly worry that his friends may be moving or have moved on. That the memory and love for Chris may be fading. But once again, these fabulous friends and family came through. They braved the chill off Lake Michigan in January to be together, to be with us, and to be with Chris. The festivities moved back to our house, Chris's house. We celebrated his life, told stories, and missed him terribly even though we felt him around us. Each of us, all of us.

CHAPTER TWO:

I'll See It When I Believe It

Note to Reader: Chris's words in his visits to me will be italicized. I have written them down verbatim. Exactly, and I mean exactly, as he sent them to me. After each visit, I labor over my hand-written messages to ensure accuracy. They will at times be grammatically incorrect, but I will not edit them. They are from my son, on the other side, and they deserve to be preserved just as he gave them to me.

ON JANUARY 28, 2018 CHRIS CAME THROUGH TO ME.

Hi Pop. Where you been? It's been a while but only the writing part. I've been around you all the time. I'm always there and always will be. You gotta accept that. 3:00 a.m. isn't the only time it's just a really good time. We can do this at different times. The energy of the darkness is conducive to clear communication. Get it? You will. I love Aunt Marcia, and she will be with me. I'm pretty powerful (not bragging) and can help her cross. Lots of family. She will be relieved. Me, I was surprised because I didn't expect it. She will feel a burden lifted and a celebration of the spirit. Hers and the family. The circle is closing.

Tell Tony thanks. Don't freak him out though. Lots of love in that painting. He loves you Pop. Lots of people do. You're special, and that's from God. I know. All love Dad. End the book on my second anniversary. There will be others.

I'll be with you in Florida at the table with the boys. Smoking a cigar & sharing love. They're great male role models. They don't realize the good they do. Al is spiritually coming into his own. I love them because they are good men. I love them because they love you. We feel that. We feel love like a vibration. Ringing, pulsating, warm. Like a giant hug. Love to hug you Pop. Always did. Strong pure hug. Good stuff. Tony has seen death and chooses gentleness and love. I'll see him again.

Mediums… they work in the spirit. That's where they are. They are conduits. They all call me. You're getting better at this Pop and I'm so proud of you.

The cleansing worked for Mom like a psychic massage. Released toxins and freed her spirit, soul, and mind. It didn't work for you. Different souls, different grade levels. But who knows? Maybe more to be revealed. Maybe not. Hey, I don't know everything, but I do know a lot, Dad. Go to the grave today and I'll meet you. I promise. Bring the dog and I'll bring God. Just fuckin' with ya. I'm humbled by the events of my anniversary. So wonderful. So much love. Good job, Dad, keep it up. Keep my name out there. Heal others Dad. Do that type of service work. It will be revealed, and you will look back & smile at me. I know this to be true.

Beaches & Boats Dad. I'm there.
Love Ya
Chris

This kid is wicked funny (that's for my Boston friends). He is sweet and witty and flat-out funny. But evidence of his advancement and growth exists on the other side. I am so friggin' proud of him and so grateful. I was never worthy of the love he had for me here, much less there. He tells me he will be there for his Aunt Marcia when she crosses (she crossed just over a year later). He talks about being with me in Florida at the annual golf trip to Loblolly Golf Club. It was just for the boys. His Uncle Mike, me, Rick Blommer or Mike Sawyer, and Allen Conrad. It was a wonderful trip full of constant golf, ball busting, cigars, steaks, and love. I am sorry that the tradition ended. But things change, don't they?

Chris makes reference to Tony (Tony Schillacci). Tony was with me since 1988 as a used car manager and was part of my career until I left the industry in 2008. I am honored to be his friend. In his youth, Tony was a highly decorated Marine. He did two tours of duty in Viet Nam and was wounded in the service of his country. He was a brilliant used car guy, a computer tech wiz, and a gifted artist. Renaissance man, anyone? No kidding. Not long after Chris's wake and funeral, I opened a package from Tony. It made my heart skip a beat and I began to cry. Tony had captured the likeness and spirit of my boy on canvas.

This framed oil painting sits on a table across from my desk. I look at it continuously every day. I even use it at times to meditate. But it all makes sense when so much love went into it.

Thanks Tony... for everything.

CHAPTER THREE:

SOMETIMES YOU DON'T HEAR THE CLICK

I do a bit of jumping around in this book. I just wrote about a session with my boy a full two years ago, and now, I'm writing about an experience that just occurred. It happens all the time actually, but usually there is a warning. In my first book, I made reference to emotional land mines. I want the parents reading this to know what they are going through is normal. God-awful painful but normal. We are walking around feeling almost whole (almost). We will never be fully whole until we are reunited with our kids on the other side. And then it hits… a song, a photo, something that triggers a memory. It's like a gut punch, I mean exactly like a gut punch.

Here's what I mean. I was coming back from having lunch with my dear friend Brad. He had picked up some kind of malady and he was down for the count for a while. On the way home, I was listening to a Mario Puzo novel. Seems safe, right? I mean, when you're listening to something about the other side or visits from passed loved ones, you are at least steeled for the likely emotional ass-kicking. But Mario Puzo? C'mon, that should be safe. Right? Being a history buff, I have read about what happens when one steps on a land mine: there is a metallic click when the trigger is depressed. The mine goes off when one removes his or her boot from the mine. Then BOOM, and all hell breaks loose. Traveling home, I hear the author discuss waking his brother and wanting to bury him the next day. So, he won't be left in the cold viewing room longer than absolutely necessary.

This passage brought me back to January 7, 2016—the day of Christopher's wake. A cold, nasty, rainy winter night where a full 2,000 friends and family members waited hours to say goodbye to Chris and express their regrets to us. The funeral parlor kept the doors open two additional hours to accommodate. A big "thank you" to funeral director Grace Martinson. The receiving line was painful but also heartwarming, each family member or friend showing love, and loss. But what killed me, absolutely killed me, was when everyone was gone, and I had to leave my Chris there for the night. It was quiet, cold, and empty. I just sat in the small sofa in front of his casket and didn't want to leave. I didn't want my boy alone. My sweet, loving, gorgeous boy. They let me stay there as long as I needed.

I don't know if I had thought of that moment in the years since his drowning. But I sure as heck am feeling it now. I've been crying on and off for a full hour. I know I'll be ok. I stopped at the market to get some groceries and picked up a dozen white roses. Right after he drowned, a wonderful medium, Nancine Meyer, told me he requested one white rose from me at his grave when we buried him on January 8. So, after dinner I will drive to Sacred Heart Cemetery with my Lab Cassidy for a visit. And I will sit beside my boy on my Buffalo Bills folding chair and have a visit. And I will bring my boy a dozen white roses. You saw that coming, didn't you? White roses, like many other objects, have become touchstones. Something that helps me connect to the other side and Chris. These objects have become precious to me and I'm sure you have your own.

EMPTY BOOTS

"My heart is broken, and it will always be broken." That is a line—it's the theme really—in the movie *Manchester by the Sea*. It's a story of loss. Loss of a child. Or in this case, children plural. I saw the movie sitting at home not long after my son Chris had drowned with his three friends in January, 2016, in a canoe accident. It always sounds silly to me to call it a canoe accident. It's not like two canoes collided on a lake. Rather, it was a perfect tragic storm. Four college boys in their early twenties, with a snoot full of alcohol jumped into a three-man canoe at 3:00 a.m. and paddled out on a partially frozen lake. They had layered clothing and untied timberland boots. None of them made it back. You probably noticed I specifically mention untied boots, which may seem a bit strange to you. But that message was given to me by a medium, not long after Chris's drowning. So, I know it's important. I know it played a part. What that part was may be revealed to me later, or maybe not. Maybe I won't know the significance until I cross over and am greeted by my boy, probably in Timberland boots, who I love and miss so terribly. At age sixty-four, that time will be sooner than later and that brings me comfort. Don't get me wrong. I'm not ready to go yet. I have work to do on this side. But the fact is my son's drowning and crossing over to the other side has changed me, forever. Mostly for the better.

I try to live a life that will make my boy proud. He has made it clear to me that I need to reach parents who have lost kids, who are going through life thinking their children's spirits died with their body. That's the lesson here. When someone dies, their spirit doesn't. But the boots did give me pause. I know this happens to you. You walk in the door and see a coat, or hear the TV and you think, "Hey, Chris is home." For a moment, just a moment, you forget your heartache and think things are back to where they were before your child crossed. Not long ago, I walked in the door and saw a pair of unlaced Timberlands and something in my soul stirred. But he wasn't home (or maybe he was) and he wasn't lounging on the couch with the remnants of a sub sandwich strewn on the coffee table. Then my heart sank, and I was back. Back to a world physically devoid of my precious Christopher. Not my favorite world, but it's the one I got.

Flash forward… April 3, 2020: Four years and three months since Christopher crossed over. I posted the above story on www. helpingparentsheal.org (a group comprised of parents who have lost children). I love that group. You can post about grief, pain, fear, and awakening without feeling judged. No one thinks the writer is looking for pity because we are all in the same boat. Occasionally, I will post something there that I wouldn't post on my own page. I received so many supportive and loving replies about the story and our book. It made the third of the month almost palatable... almost.

Because the weather was pretty mild for April, I was meeting my son Will at our golf club to sneak out and play a round. In the Jeep, I received a call from Sheri Jewel, my medium pal. She had given my name to a client who had recently lost an adult child and wanted to give me a heads-up. As we continued to chat, she said she felt Chris around her by a tingle on the crown of her head. Yep, she said. He's here. She told me Chris was confirming he's always around me and always will be. Sheri asked if I recently felt some perceived distance and was worried about separation. She asked me if I recently requested a sign. I told her yes and yes.

A short time ago, I had asked Chris for a sign and expected a red cardinal to cross my path. But my boy is nothing if not unpredictable. Sheri told me Chris is showing her Timberland boots. She asked if that meant anything to me. You need to understand, Sheri has not lost a child and is not privy to that website. She knows nothing about me writing and then posting the story at 8:45 a.m. that morning. She was only sharing what Chris was showing her. I started to cry and felt a rush of joy and love all over. She said Chris was smiling a sideways smile, "almost like a smirk." He's really happy. And he's surrounded by a whole group of friends. He's good. Did he like whiskey sours? I had to laugh, because he did in fact drink whiskey sours. I'm not sure why that always struck me as funny, but it did. And I know he's running it by as an affirmation.

Although it was the third of the month, Chris made me feel light as a feather (another sign from him) and happy. If you have any doubts about spirit and the other side, then explain this one to me. I've written this down just the way it happened. No embellishment, no bullshit.

If you are still hanging in there with me, you deserve an explanation. How can your son drown in a canoe in 2016 and then appear to a medium four years and three months later? Well, it's simple… sort of.

The best explanation about what happens when your soul leaves your body comes from a movie, *What Dreams May Come*. In the film, Cuba Gooding plays a spirit guide to the recently deceased doctor portrayed brilliantly by Robin Williams. He explains it this way: *"The origin of the word "body" is the Anglo-Saxon "bodig" meaning abode. Which is what the physical body is, you see. A transient dwelling for the real self. Like you're in your house right now. You're in your house, that doesn't mean you are your house. House falls down, you get out and walk away."*

This is so simply put, so clarifying. And it makes total sense. We need to separate who we are—our soul, our spirit—from our body, which is a temporary structure housing our true self. When I finally grasped this concept, a whole lot shifted in my world. It all started to make sense.

This knowing is a magnificent revelation. But it doesn't take the pain away. Anyone who tells you that "time heals all wounds" hasn't lost a child. The same way anyone who tells you, "I lost a sibling, a parent, or a cat, so I know what you're going through" hasn't lost a child. It's grueling. It's a club nobody ever wants to join. But in my case, the horrific loss—the hole in me—has propelled me on a spiritual path, which will culminate in a reunion with my son, and my sister, and my parents, and all my siblings on the other side. And how in God's (literally) name do I know of this upcoming homecoming? I have been told by my son that this is what will happen. So, I know it to be true.

ON FEBRUARY 10, 2018 CHRIS CAME THROUGH.

Hi Dad, I'm still here. Love you Dad. I was with you at Scotty's lake house. You don't need to go back. You answered the call but I'm not there. My spirit left there that day. I went with you to the lake. You need to stay close for this to work. Stay in both of our worlds. Yours is so temporary that you will be pissed you were focusing on it. Trust me… there you go. Get back to the Source. I'm the one who found the account to allow you to relax. Don't be so attached to worldly things and then cross the bridge to visit. Get it? Only God's world, my world, is everlasting. I miss you too, so dive in Dad. Get deeper Dad. Go Sunday to the group. I'll be there. Let go, full in. Work on it.

Love ya

Let's talk about this. When I am entering this dialogue into this book it's two years after it has taken place. It's also two years since I've reviewed the conversation or notes. There is a sentence preceding *you answered the call*. But I can't decipher it. So, it's omitted. There is also a bit of a story about my visit to the lake on February 9, 2018. That was just over two years since the drowning. I was in the northern suburbs visiting a client. I noticed I wasn't far from the Wisconsin border and Lake Beulah. Something called me to visit the lake when my visit was concluded. I did. I knew the house would be vacant as it was a beach house, a summer residence. The family who owned it would be home in Wilmette.

It was painful. As I pulled into the driveway, all the memories of January 3, 2016 came flooding back. The sights, the sounds, the heartbreak. It was winter and the ground was covered with snow. But since my business for the day was concluded, the worst I could expect was wet shoes, socks, and pant legs for an uncomfortable ride home. The ride home was going to be uncomfortable anyway, so I didn't really care. I walked past the house and down the hill through the backyard to the water's edge. I looked back and saw the picture window I had looked out through over the lake two years before. Jesus (not cursing) this was hard. I looked at the lake where the canoe had been overturned and where the recovery boats took its place. I stood silently and told my boy I loved and missed him, and I cursed the lake. Next, I turned around and headed the fifty or so yards back to my Jeep. It was only then that I noticed despite walking in a foot of snow, my shoes and pant legs were perfectly dry; I swear to you people, they weren't even damp.

Currently, we are discussing a screenplay for *My Search...*, and someone involved brought up some mild embellishment to make the story more attractive to the audience. My answer was firm and final. I would set fire to any screenplay that wasn't 100 percent factual. My goodness... after reading the last story, how could one even find a way to embellish that occurrence?

In his visit, Chris talks about a fund account he pointed me to that I had lost track of. I hadn't really forgotten about it, but I was surprised by the balance. Still too embedded in the affairs of this world, I believe it brought me comfort. Don't get me wrong, I'm not like Scrooge McDuck but a few extra shekels can always come in handy on this side.

The next day, I attended a spirit circle with my medium pal Sheri Jewel. I love Sheri, but hate groups. But I attended as I was instructed to do so by my boy. Chris, of course, came through as he always did with Sheri. She told me he was there with a dog that had previously passed. That was Casey. She was an eighty-pound yellow Lab that thought Christopher was her pup. Once, when Chris was about two years old, we attended a pool party nearby. Although we kept a close eye on our busy, young boy as he was constantly in motion, we actually could have relaxed because Casey was on the job. She would put herself between her beloved Christopher and the pool whenever he was on the move. So, of course it made sense she was with him. When Casey was fourteen and her body was failing, we had to put her down. Chris refused to allow us to do it without him. The three of us—Chris, Sally, and I—held and kissed Casey as she crossed over. It only makes sense that numerous mediums have told me Chris was greeted by a big white dog (very light-yellow actually) when he crossed. And it makes sense they are together. Love never dies. I read that somewhere. Oh yeah, it's my publisher's tag line. Sheri also told me he mentioned a car accident of his and that I should trust the journey and he was always going to be with me. Maybe I should stop whining about being part of a group. My boy came through; that's all I needed.

ON FEBRUARY 14, 2018, ST. VALENTINE'S DAY, CHRIS VISITED.

Hi Dad,

Happy Valentine's Day. Another year, another day, all the same. You'll see. I called you, I reached out to you. This is why it works, so don't sweat the time in between. Because time doesn't exist. One continual visit. Feel me around your neck. That tingle is all me Pop. You know that. So beautiful here. Soft blue and greens like nothing you've ever seen. Even though it's the same colors on your side, the colors take on a whole new meaning here. Work on the book ("My Search") this weekend. I'll be with you to help. Strong connection today. I know you are worried but now you can relax. As much as you can relax. You crack me up. But I sure do love you. It's part of you and I love it. Because it's you. If you are stopping by the grave bring a shovel cuz snow is deep. I'd come to visit but I'm on the beach not in the snow… would you? Good meditation—I chose it for you. I'm pushing some buttons where I can. Believe it.

I love the portrait, my spirit is in the portrait. You are moving toward the light. Toward my world. But it's not now. You're not ready. But you will be. I'll get you there. Flowers Pop, soft & beauty. (not a typo—how it was written). This every day. It really is paradise. See a cardinal? It's me.

Good progress Pop. You've pushed through a level. Really great. I'm here. The tingle is all over now, not just the neck. New level, new opening. Great to hug you, right over left. Not sure, whatever Pop. No worries. So many times, just you and me and they all come to me on recall. So clear. So loving. They are pleased at what you are doing. Keep it up. Feel the tingle and look for the red birds. Me touching you from this side. Break through Pop. We are back connected even stronger. The love is forever, so is the connection. Let it flow over you. It will always be that way until we are together again.

So much love Pop
C

Chris tells me they are pleased about what I am doing. I think I know who they are. I will find out eventually.

Later that morning, Sally called to tell me that while in the Starbucks drive-thru, a cardinal landed on her Jeep. She knew what it meant. Happy Valentine's Day, Momma.

FEBRUARY 28, 2018

Hi Pop. Where ya been? You getting old? No problem. I'm here. I love the sand. Things are getting done with Will. That's good. I'm there. I'll help. He'll be o.k.

Get more in my world. You're getting comfortable. Get the book finished. It's my book Dad. It won't mean connection is less. More doors on my side will open. You'll see. My friends still make me happy with plans for my birthday. I'm still with them. Maybe they will start feeling me as they open up. Get to a beach Pop. Marcia is near. Jerry is waiting for her and so am I. It will complete the circle. One opening when you join us but that's down the road Pop. You have work to do.

Back of the neck Pop. That's the spot. I'm here. Get deeper. I'll do the rest. Remember when I was happy at the Ranch? That's all the time now. Always fit in. Always loved. Always accepted.

I'm pushing for the blood stone. Get one today. I'll be there to pick it out. I'll even drive with you. The writing will flow and I'll take it from there. The music is for you and me. The book is for others. Do service to those with broken hearts. Their loved ones are knocking on their door. Help them open up Pop.

Your dad is here. I mean, right here. I love that guy and he loved you. Still does. I'm as close as the picture. Raise your energy and stay open. Trust the flow. I always listened but I didn't always hear you. But now I can see every conversation as pure love from you. I am really impressed by how much you loved me & still do. Thanks Pop, thanks Dad. There isn't time but the family is closer because of Marcia's energy. I'm guiding her on your side. Exit points Pop. You'll get it. Maybe not now.

Another pub crawl on my birthday. I'm honored. And you can be present because you're not hosting it. Just love them for me and

*you. Thanks for waking up Pop. The 3:00 a.m. alarm, that's me
Pop. I feel it all.*

*I'm glad my dog is there with you. I'm hanging with Casey.
She loved you so much too. And me. Me more now Pop.*

*Heading Back
Love you
Chris*

Well, another wonderful visit with Chris. He mentions he loves
the sand. After writing in my first book about the sand (which
is not sand but rather quartz crystal) of Siesta Key, my pal Jeff
brought me a small jar of sand from there on his next visit. I
keep a steady supply of this crystal on my desk and spread it on
my legal pad during my meditation and his downloads. Quit
rolling your eyes and read below.

Siesta Key sand is so soft. The sand is made of ninety-nine percent pure quartz crystal mineral, ultimately derived from the Southern Appalachian Mountains. Over many, many years the mineral grains were carried by rivers into the Gulf and further south along the Florida coastline.

This is the stuff rituals are made of. It works, Chris likes it, it's in for good. He mentions his friends, who were preparing for the Second Chris McQ Pub Crawl on his birthday. He tells me maybe they will start feeling him as they "open up." Stay tuned. He tells me I needn't worry that the finishing of *My Search...* wouldn't end our connection. It's a forever thing. He tells me Marcia is near. I know my beloved sister is on her last lap around the track (not that she ever ran around a track in her life) and that she would be coming home soon. He mentions Jerry waiting for her. I know how much she missed her older brother and best friend Jerry who crossed over on June 21, 2014. Christopher went to Jerry's funeral with me in Boston and spent the entire time taking care of his wheelchair-bound Godmother Aunt Marcia. He was so tender and so sweet. I was so proud of him. I was even proud of him when he decided to pick up the entire bar bill at the hotel for my family and charge it to the room. It was just what his Uncle Jerry would have done. Or he would have split it with me. But Jerry wasn't there for me to split it with. So, when Chris came up to the room and explained what he did with the bar bill, I just had to smile. The kid had style. Chris says that Marcia crossing will complete a circle that will open up when I cross. That is very comforting to me knowing they will all be there.

Chris also mentions a blood stone. And that's a little foggy to me. I had a blood stone I either lost or gave away. I went back to a crystal store on Western Avenue to get another, but it was closed after many years. The owner himself had crossed over.

Chris mentions my dad. He tells me how much my dad always loved me. I knew he loved me even when he wouldn't approve or condone my behavior as a rebellious young man. The confidence I derived from being loved helped me back then, and does to this day. If I wanted approval, I need only do things worthy of approval, right? But I never doubted my parents' love.

Christopher's Godfather Uncle Mike's cousin Darcy quoted something about this fact, and it was perfect. I asked her to write it down. I keep it taped on my wall above a painting of a cardinal: *"The unassailable self-confidence that comes from a childhood insulated with love."*

That's it, that's the magic formula. That's why I knew I could push the envelope and always come home. Very early on Nancine told me that about Chris. She actually said he talked about being comfortable enough to "push the envelope." He knew he was loved. We both know we are still loved. Knowing Chris is with my father is very comforting to me. Many mediums, from Concetta Bertoldi, to Andrew Anderson, to Sheri Jewel, all mention my dad in the readings. They say he stays back in the background adding support for Chris and me. In one reading with Sheri Jewel, my dad stepped forward, put his arm around Chris, and told me, "Don't worry… I got the kid." He couldn't be in better hands.

As for today, Chris mentions that when he was at the Ranch, he was happy. He tells me that's how every day is with him now. He's always happy. I know if you are reading this you are worried about someone on the other side. How are they now? Was their passing traumatic? Maybe they weren't happy when they crossed over but I promise you they are now. You'll see.

He tells me he is happy his dog was with me in my office during our session. Cassidy is often my late-night companion during meditation and at the grave. He also mentions our Lab

Casey, who is with him now. And she loves me, he tells me. But not, according to Chris, as much as she now loves him. I get it, buddy.

MARCH 14, 2018

That day in Iowa. That snapshot was a snapshot of us. Still us. One energy. Glad you're back on track Dad. The healing was good. Trust me and have faith that he's right about water. It's like fuel. But it cleans you out. You are starting to get that too. Keep doing good work and the heavens open up. Even the little things you do make a mark. It's a channel. I'm good. Finding my pace. I'm finally a student.

We're together Pop. But I like the grave too. Spring is coming. My friends planning the crawl, that makes me smile. It keeps me connected too. Stones, music, sage… They aren't just props. It's energy, it's real. Keep one foot in each world. The book will end with the second anniversary of my crossing. But you and I will always dialogue. You will always journal it. That's how we will always communicate.

I really don't know if seeing me is in the cards but keep pushing. My spot, my energy, it matters. Feel the Sarasota sand. A sacred place. Full of messengers and messages in the life. In the coming days be wide open. I'm here Dad. Your soul's opening up. Like a door. A little at first and then Wham… Make it Big (just fucking with you). Can you see my sideways smile Pop? I'm smiling at you. The music, the dog. Breathe that life in and out.

I'm pushing Will. Keep on him but don't worry so much. Even about finances. It will all flow. Trust me. You can count on me. I put together the lacrosse net, didn't I? ☺ It's funny, I miss my Jeep. Even though I can do and go anywhere over here.

I miss you Pop. You'll always be my dad no matter. Like Arizona. Such a short life. Such a short run.

But you will be with me here & it's impossible to describe how great it is. You'll get here, and you'll get it. I know. Get to the beach as soon as it warms up & I'll be there next to you.

Love
Chris

Holy smokes… where do I start? That day in Iowa. Chris, Caroline, and I went to Ames, Iowa for my niece Jamie's wedding in October of 2014. The afternoon of the wedding we were at a street fair, just hanging out. Just being. I always said we could just *be* together. Chris mentions "one energy," and that's exactly how it felt. Later on, in my journey, I had a medium mention Chris and I were "twin flames"—a term I'd never heard of. I looked it up and it made total sense. Katherine Hurst defines it like this:

WHAT IS A TWIN FLAME?

Sometimes discussed in terms of a "mirror soul" or "soul connection," a twin flame is the other half of your soul. It is theorized that a soul can split into two after ascending to a high frequency. Thereafter, the soul lands in two different bodies.

If you compare a twin flame vs. soulmate, it's important to note that a soul mate is someone who is made from the same kind of energy as you, but who has never existed in fusion with you. So, although soulmate connections are highly significant, an encounter with a twin flame is on another level entirely.

I love that… I mean I really love that! I have a Yankee Candle on my desk with two wicks, representing twin flames. You probably would have figured that out by yourself. I love the reinforcement that we are more than kindred spirits. We are actually two spirits sharing one soul. The picture really says a lot. And it brings me comfort and often to tears at the same time. If you're a parent, you get it. I write music with a dear pal Brad Nye. He is a big part of my life and a big help with everything artistically. He sent me the opening chords of a song about grief. We knocked it out in twenty minutes with Chris at my side. We recorded it with Brad and the brilliant guitarist Mike Aquino. You can hear it along with the other songs we've recorded as a tribute to Chris, here: https://soundcloud.com/tributetochrismcquillen

Old Grief and Love
No that ain't a tear in my eye
It's just the wind blowin' by
Let's chalk it up to one nice try
That's old grief and love

How could I've known, when I made the deal
That in the end this is how I'd feel
But one thing's sure the hurt is real
That's just old grief and love
You never know what will start the slide
A baseball glove, or a pony ride, a picture of you and me side by side
So much love and now it's gone
You drink, you curse you write a song
You hold on waiting for the dawn
With old grief and love
You never know what will start the slide
A puppy dog or a pony ride, a picture of you and me side by side
How can you know, what I'm trying to say, that old grief he visits every day
I'm thinking that he's here to stay, that's old grief and love
I'm guessing that's he's here to stay, that's just old grief and love.

That song was inspired by grief and the picture of Chris and me side by side. That photo—from a family wedding in Ames, Iowa—is never far from my memory. I just shut my eyes and it's there.

The wedding in Ames also brings a memory that will stay with me forever. The reception was in full swing and there was a carefree joy permeating the entire room. Our family, the McQuillen clan, was represented by family members from all over the country. Chris, Caroline, and I attended as Sally and Will were at a lacrosse tourney. Like most parents with these special moments, I remember every detail of the trip. Every moment. I picked up Caroline at the train station, picked up Chris in DeKalb, we stopped at Five Guys for a burger, and we headed to Iowa. From the minute we arrived Chris was immersed in family, in just being. Being an accepted, valued, loved member of the family. In Ames, we took over a local pancake house (as only McQuillens could do), went to a street fair, and hung out. The reception was held at a lovely winery in the late afternoon. When the dancing began, I sat back and watched my kids. I viewed them not as individuals but rather as members of a loving group. It was magical (I can't believe I just used that term). But it was. As a father, and member of the clan as well, I was just overwhelmed by joy, and love. At one point, I looked out on the dance floor and saw my beautiful son surrounded by family, his family, hula girl tie askew, dancing and singing "Wagon Wheel." I smiled—hell, I beamed. And someone captured it with a photo. Only later, upon viewing the picture after Chris had crossed over did the quote from *A River Runs Through It* come to me. In the movie/book, Norman MacLean was looking at his brother fly-fishing. He was beautiful and almost perfect in that moment and I knew exactly what he meant when he said: *"And I knew just as surely, just as clearly, that life is not a work of art, and that the moment could not last."*

By the way...it isn't, and it doesn't. Our band, Frat Dog, covers "Wagon Wheel" at the golf outing concert. And it brings us all joy, and some of us tears.

Chris talks a lot about energy... so I know it's important. The stones and sage, he tells me, aren't just props. He talks about sacred places. I also refer to them as "thin places." Places where the veil is thinnest between our worlds. I know it's very thin on Lido and Siesta Keys in Florida, for example. And to a little lesser degree, Naples and Vanderbilt Beach. Sacred Heart Cemetery is a thin place for me. Especially at night. I have visited some other sacred or thin places in my pursuit of the Other Side, some that moved me and some that didn't. Hang in there. We'll get there.

Chris talks about the fact that we will continue to dialogue. He also lightens things up with his humor. He talks about the door to the knowledge of the other side opening up... and then, "Wham!" Make it Big. The album, get it? He does crack me up still, and he knows it. He acknowledges his pals planning the second pub crawl on his birthday. I've been asked if I thought spirits miss things. And he flat-out confirms it. He misses his Jeep Wrangler. Why am I not surprised? But then he says he misses me, too. Which makes me smile and cry just a little. He tells me to just trust what he's telling me. He mentions the lacrosse net. Let me explain. I had bought Will a lacrosse net and it was no surprise to anyone who knows me that I was struggling with the assembly. Chris had just pulled up with his pal Nick, and relieved me of the duty. It was up and operating in no time. So, yeah buddy, you did handle that task. And you handle a whole lot more still from your side.

ON MARCH 22, 2018, CHRIS CAME THROUGH.

It's a door Dad. When the time comes you just walk through it. You won't be freaked out or afraid, because of all the time we've spent. As soon as you walk through the door I'll be there. Sorry I had to leave and it's hard for you to know but it was for the best. But I miss you too & I am sorry for the pain. The pain would have been worse though. Let it go Dad.

Nice meditation this morning. You're starting to see me in your head. That's a good start. You always made me feel safe and I'm grateful. About military school. Let it go. Guilt is wasted and so outweighed by the eternal love you brought and still bring to me. Get the cardinal tattoo. I absolutely approve it Pop. Keep your head up. I'm on it. You've run a good race and I won't let you down. You can count on me. You and me Dad. Calling you Dad because I'm feeling very close and loved. Like the old days (for you). Time is different here. Not even going to try and describe it. It's home here, and it will be for you. But not now… not yet. No pain on my end Pop. Just love. You always cried when I left for Tucson and I always knew, and it made me feel loved. Thanks for that. But the best thing you ever did was be a great dad. Loved & kept safe. I feel that on my side all the time. See the beach Dad? I'm not restless, I'm at peace. You will be too. I'm trying to bring that to you on your side.

Hi Dad. That's my voice.
Love you Dad and I'll be with you today.
Love you
Chris

Well that's amazing. How much clearer can Chris make it? When the time comes, you walk through it. This is a wonderful visit yet in some ways a very tough read for me. Chris talks about the timing of his crossing over. He tells me he had to leave when he did, that life would have been much harder for him going forward if he hadn't. That just flat-out breaks my heart. And deserved or not, I feel like I failed him. Here is how the author Amanda Linette Meder describes the process in her book, *Crossing Over*.

> **Crossing Over** is a term that is used to describe an event in which someone, generally a living person or animal, leaves their physical body and the physical earth and transcends as an eternal Spirit into the Spirit World.
>
> The idea here is that you are a soul in a physical body, and when your physical body ceases to operate, the Soul (or Spirit) continues to exist elsewhere. In this sense, there are two worlds where we, as souls in physical bodies can exist: the physical, tangible world and there is the spiritual, intangible world. When the physical body is lost in death, the majority of people leave their bodies behind as cohesive Spirits and return to the Spirit World.
>
> The Spirit World is also referred to as Heaven, the Other Side, the After Life, Source, the Universal Eden, so on and so forth. I will be using the terms Other Side and After Life primarily in this eBook. However, all terms are used to describe the same place—the place where our Spirit goes when the physical body ceases to function and also, returns to Earth.

During this visit, Chris tells me to get the cardinal tattoo. No if, ands, or buts. So, I do. On May 14, just over a month and a half after his message, I visited Dave McNair, my old friend from Chicago Tattoo and had a beautiful red cardinal tattooed on my right forearm. I'm so happy I did it. It's a constant reminder (not that I need one) of my boy.

Chris also tells me, "You've run a good race and I won't let you down." This means the world to me, because he approves of how I'm living my life. He's proud of his old man. It was when reflecting on this visit that I was brought back to his funeral and the reading from *Timothy*, Chapter 4, Verse 6–8: "I am already being poured out like a libation, and the time of my departure is at hand. I have competed well; I have finished the race; I have kept the faith."

I can't ask for a better affirmation from my boy than that. When my time comes, I'll just walk through the door. Just like Chris has told me.

Also, in this visit, as you could see in his message, he talks about the guilt I carry about military school. Let me tell you about this chapter in our lives.

In 2008, Chris was fourteen years old and a handful. He was rebellious, a bit out of control. I was working 'round the clock and his mom couldn't even get him to go to school. He was drinking and experimenting with drugs. Even our connection that was always so strong was strained. It was hard on us all.

The summer before, we sent him to camp at a military school an hour away in Wisconsin. He thrived there, loving the physical activity and the challenges. His positive experience there gave us hope and we decided to send him to St. John's Northwestern Military Academy (SJNMA) in the fall. Well, you can imagine how that worked out. He had learning disabilities and the school was not equipped to deal with those.

Of course, at school he gravitated toward the other malcontents and it was a disaster. We would drive up to watch his JV football games and seeing how unhappy our son was, we would come home—after an extremely short interaction (the Academy's rules) with our unhappy son—just heartbroken. It wasn't a good fit. During a semester break, Chris didn't want to come home because he felt having to leave to go back to school would be too difficult. So, I booked a suite at a hotel in Milwaukee for the two of us. We ate well, binge-watched hotel movies, went to a Milwaukee Brewers convention (where I bought him a light-blue hoodie he wore for years after), and even took in a Milwaukee Bucks basketball game. I cherished every single minute. I can even tell you two of the movies we watched: *Pineapple Express* and *Role Models*.

Trying to touch all the bases I even booked a suite with a hot tub. I noticed that Chris had a couple of half-moon scars on his arm. I asked him about those and he didn't want to talk about it. I didn't want to press the topic. He was as happy as he'd been since first leaving home and I didn't want to disrupt that mood.

Halfway into the week-long break, he asked if we could go home for the remainder of the time. We packed up within minutes and headed south to Winnetka. When we got home, his mother was beside herself with joy. She so loved her boy. When Sally took in her beautiful son, she noticed what I considered the small scar or scars. Over the next couple of days, she wormed (operative word here) the story out of him. He told her he had been held down and branded by members of a Latino gang called the El Presidentes. Sally was furious, heartbroken, and guilt-ridden. What sort of place had we sent him to? To whom did we turn over the care of our son?

The next day, I called the president of the school and made an appointment. I shared our tale and advised he bring his check-book and have his attorney on speed dial (remember speed dial?).

He asked that we schedule the meeting in few days to allow him to do a thorough investigation into the incident.

On the morning of the meeting, I checked in on my sleeping

boy, kissed him lightly on the forehead, and headed north to slay the dragon. When I arrived, the mood wasn't what I'd anticipated. What I expected was coffee and Danishes on a wheeled serving cart, board members shifting nervously from one foot to the other, and a large, leather-bound, ledger-style checkbook with a shark's tooth check just awaiting an amount to be filled in (by fountain pen, btw). That's not what I got... not any of it.

The president, sitting perfectly erect, attired in a three-piece suit, welcomed me curtly into his office and pointed to a chair. He then began to tell me his version of the story after his investigation. St. John's Military Academy had a large number of foreign students, many from prestigious Mexican families, with sons of high-ranking military, political, and diplomatic members. The El Presidentes were a group of Mexican honor students from these ranks. Furthermore, what the investigation uncovered was that a number of knuckleheaded cadets (like Chris) were bored and decided to see who could keep a flame-heated penny on their arm the longest. This resulted in the crescent-shaped scars on his and his pals' arms. This meeting was not going as anticipated; there was no coffee, Danishes, check, or apology forthcoming. I stood up, nodded my understanding, tucked my tail beneath my dark Brooks Brothers suit, and scurried from the room.

When I arrived home from the Academy after an hour-plus drive, I walked down to the basement where Chris was lounging on the couch, wrapped up in a blanket watching a sitcom. "Well," he said to me, hopefully, "how did it go?" and that was that. We didn't send him back. Even though we were out a year's tuition, we were relieved and grateful to have our boy home. Life's a funny old thing. I should have been mad, and I know I was briefly. But it was the first time I felt whole in a number of months. The other part of my soul, my twin flame, was back under my roof. At least temporarily.

CHAPTER FOUR:

NEAR-DEATH EXPERIENCES

On April 2, 2018, I awoke at 3:00 a.m. more awake than usual. In Chris's room, I set up for the meditation—candles, sage, pictures—and began to listen to a guided meditation. Then... nothing. I felt a little tingle on the back of my neck and again... nothing. I waited, blew out the candles, turned off the meditation, and went back to our bedroom.

In bed, I turned on the TV to help me fall back to sleep and a movie called *Hereafter* was on. Directed by Clint Eastwood, it was a film about three people; a grieving boy, a psychic, and a woman who had a near-death experience (NDE) and wrote a book. I really believed that Chris held back that morning so I would watch it. Why? I don't know. But I have faith it will be revealed. The movie was just ok. Not a lot of depth (sorry Clint). I felt the movie just skimmed the surface of NDEs and the psychic. There didn't appear to be a lot of research behind it. Upon thinking about a lesson that might be in it for me, I realized the woman with the NDE, who was writing a book about her experience, recognized she needed to find a publisher that understood her experience. Hmmm, good advice.

I have yet to have a NDE. But having researched them (mostly while researching the afterlife—the end destination, as it were), I am a total believer. The consistencies of the stories by those reporting first-hand are undeniable. It's amazing how many doctors (M.D.s, not witchdoctors) who experience a soul's return to the body, are not only converts but have written their own accounts. One of my favorites is *To Heaven and Back*, by Mary C. Neal, MD. It's her own story of her soul leaving and returning after a visit to heaven. But I bet you guessed that. Her story touched my soul on a number of levels (I mention her again a bit more in a few pages, so keep reading!). Another book written not through personal experience but rather through research and interviews is *Imagine Heaven*, by John Burke. Burke tells the story in a way that's easy to comprehend... and believe.

When it comes to NDEs, there are first-person and third-person accounts; the first-person is personal experience, the third-person is reporting another's experience of story. See below... (you're welcome).

- First-, second-, and third-person are ways of describing points of view.
- First-person is the I/we perspective.
- Second-person is the you perspective.
- Third-person is the he/she/it/they perspective.

So, let me explain. When I finished the manuscript for *My Search for Christopher on the Other Side*, I assumed this groundbreaking story of connecting with the afterlife would take the world by storm. I mean, nobody could have experienced what I have and then reported back, could they? Well yes, lots of people. And, there were plenty of books on the subject. Some were very good, some were not. Some rang true to my experience and some seemed like new-age bull hockey. I have had the same experience with books on NDEs; many of the books on NDEs written by doctors are dry and clinical (not Mary C. Neal, MD's, btw). Others are frilly and quite honestly neither relatable nor believable. In fact, many of the silly frilly reports were prior to what I believe is a new-age awakening we are now experiencing. If you start to read a chapter or two of a book on NDEs and you find yourself falling asleep, drooling on the pages, or grimacing in discomfort, put the book down. Go to Amazon, or even better visit a local book store (but not the Bookstall in Winnetka—they wouldn't carry my book), and peruse NDEs. Just look at the stories and I promise one will grab your attention. Spirit will help… is that too frilly? Well, get over it because that's how it works.

What exactly is a NDE? Defining a near-death experience is tricky, because it's other things to other people. Some claim it is actually death and then a return to life. Others believe it's a brush with death. One thing is certain: it is now widely accepted as fact. There have been way too many reports from medical personnel witnessing those events and way too many reports of the return to the body in the first-person to ever dismiss it as a hoax or a hallucination. It's real, it happens. But NDEs are not the only experiences; they are joined by NDLEs and NDAs.

So, what are they? The Eternea (the homepage for The Convergence of Science and Spirituality for Personal & Global Transformation) describes a near-death experience as follows:

"A near-death experience (NDE) is a spiritual, transcendental or other-worldly event that can occur during a clinical, imminent or possibly imminent death situation. The NDE can also occur while suffering from trauma or while having an intense desire to die."

Here is a list of what one commonly experiences during a NDE. I have gleaned these from a number of sources, including the Eternea:

- An experience or feeling of intense peace
- A feeling of oneness with everything
- A sense of knowing everything
- Receiving messages in telepathic form
- Having a sense or awareness of being dead
- Having a sense of well-being and painlessness; positive emotions
- An out-of-body experience. A perception of one's own body from an outside position or perspective. Witnessing earthly events or people when out of the body.
- A sense of moving up, or through, a tunnel
- An awareness or sudden immersion in a powerful light. Communication with the light.
- An intense feeling of unconditional love
- Encountering "Beings of Light"
- Encountering or feeling reunited with deceased loved ones or with one's soul family
- Being given a life review, where one's own life events are viewed or relived (this is only experienced by people over the age of six years)
- A decision by oneself or others to return to one's body, often accompanied by a reluctance to return
- Encountering spiritual beings
- Seeing a brilliant landscape with enhanced senses. Vibrant colors beyond description upon return.

This is a pretty comprehensive list, which seems to touch a lot of the basics. For more information on NDEs, go to the Appendix at the end of this book.

Also related to NDEs and actual dying, is the concept of life reviews. Let me share a bit more to help you see what I'm writing about. While researching this book, I have read countless encounters just like the ones that follow.

In filmmaker Craig McMahon's series of films, *Life to Afterlife*, the subjects in his latest piece, *Life to Afterlife: Death and Back,* discuss all aspects of dying, including life review. McMahon is an amazing filmmaker and even a better guy, and his films have given me answers to many questions. We all believe, or in my case know, we have a life review after we cross. The description of this review by Craig's subject Erika was so revealing and reassuring it brought tears to my eyes. Erika's story let me know I'm on the right path. She tells us there are two reviews; one is like a film reel of your life, and one is about all the loving impact you have had on others (whether you're aware of it or not). God actually dropped a rock in a body of water as an example of the ripple effect your actions have had on others during the second review with Erika.

I have written before about Christopher's kindness to the less fortunate and it's inspired me. I do things that I know make Christopher proud and I don't discuss them with others. I'm not looking for credit. I'm only telling you now as an example.

A few months back, I passed a woman on the highway who was pulled over. Let's be clear: I passed her and it began to gnaw on me. I got off the next exit and circled back. Sure enough, she was out of coolant and asked if I had any water. I drove to the nearest gas station and bought some coolant and a funnel. I wouldn't hear of her paying me back, as this was a gift. Actually, a gift to Chris.

More recently, just few days ago, as I was approaching an exit to pick up dinner at a local Italian beef stand, I passed a woman pulled over in obvious distress. This time, I only had to back up. Albeit on the highway. She was in a van and one of her kids had left her gas tank empty. When I approached, she was so grateful because her only source of help was a brother who drove a truck and was in Michigan. I had her jump in and took the same exit we were headed to and bought a gas can and a gallon of gas. This time, she paid as I didn't want to insult her. We filled the can, circled back to the highway, and pulled behind her van. We began to put gas in her car when an emergency transportation truck pulled behind and assisted in the filling. The spouts on new gas cans are pretty complicated. She started her van and after thanking me profusely, she was on her way. Because the safety truck pulled up right after we returned, this meant she wasn't going to be stranded even if I hadn't stopped. However, I felt it was far from a wasted effort.

In both cases I've outlined, my assisting told someone in need that people are kind and really do care, even if helping is inconvenient. It also fills my spirit. It washes away some of the stain of selfishness that has built up over my lifetime. I also know it makes my son Chris proud. He knows this change in me was brought about by his inspiration. And for a kicker, it appears these acts of kindness will show up on my second life review. So, any inconvenience to me is a small price to pay.

There is one case, reported by author Kimberly Sharp Clark, where a patient had a near-death experience while being resuscitated. She told a nurse she saw a blue gym shoe, or sneaker on a third-floor ledge of the hospital. The patient said it was a left gym shoe with a worn toe. This part of the roof was nowhere near her line of sight. The nurse told a resident, who in turn had someone search the third floor's ledges. Sure enough, that person returned from the other side of the hospital with a blue gym shoe (left foot) with a worn toe exactly as described by the patient.

There are countless instances of patients reporting leaving their body and floating up, looking down at the staff in the hospital rooms. They have actually reported conversations between the medical personnel, that they observed from their vantage point above while in a coma or even while dead. Such instances have apparently become commonplace. One such occurrence shared by author John Burke, a skeptic-turned-believer, was a report by a NDE client completely under sedation recalling one surgeon not wearing shoe covers, but instead wearing white patent leather shoes (spiffy). That particular surgeon wasn't in attendance before or after surgery; only when the patient was completely under sedation and redlining.

In another NDE instance, a doctor—Dr. Richard Eby—was dead for ten hours. He plunged two stories to a concrete sidewalk below. While dead, he encountered all of the experiences that accompany a visit to the other side—the vibrant colors, the wisdom, the love. But what impacted him most when reporting upon his return was that the Supreme Being or Creator knew his name. "Dick," the voice said, "you're dead." It was decided that Richard's work on this side was not done and he returned, waking up in the morgue a full ten hours after the accident.

And while we're on the topic of physicians reporting their own NDEs, I come back to physician-author Dr. Mary C. Neal, whose name I mentioned earlier. Dr. Neal is a board-certified orthopedic spine surgeon who drowned while kayaking on a South American river. She experienced life after death. She went to heaven and back, conversed with Jesus, and experienced God's encompassing love. She was returned to Earth with some specific instructions for work she still needed to do. Her life has been one filled with the miracles and intervention of God. Her story gives reason to live by faith and is a story of hope (NDEstories.org).

Dr. Neal's amazing book, *To Heaven and Back*, will give you hope, and break your heart. But it happened, I know in my heart, just as she wrote it did. What brought me the most peace, other than another amazing validation of life after life, was her description of drowning. Here is an excerpt from her book:

> I wasn't screaming, and really wasn't feeling any pain. I felt curiously blissful.
> This is quite a remarkable statement considering I had always been terrified of drowning. While my body was being slowly sucked out of the boat, I felt as though my soul was slowly peeling itself away from my body. I finally felt my body release from the boat and begin to tumble with the current. That was the last physical sensation I had with regard to my body. I do not remember scraping along the bottom of the river, bumping into Chad, or being pulled to the river bank.
> At the moment my body was released and began to tumble, I felt a "pop." It felt as if I had finally shaken off my heavy outer layer, freeing my soul. I rose up and out of the river, and when my soul broke through the surface of the water, I encountered a group of fifteen to twenty souls (human spirits sent by God), who greeted me with the most overwhelming joy I have ever experienced and could ever imagine.
>
> (*To Heaven and Back* (pp. 68-70).
> The Crown Publishing Group. Kindle Edition.)

When I got to this part of her book, I began to weep. I mean, really weep. You see, Chris drowned and although we had been told by numerous sources, including mediums, that his death was painless, here was an actual account of drowning. By someone who had actually drowned. And she was using terms like 'curiously blissful' to describe her process. Sally and I never talked about it, but we were and sometimes still are haunted by Chris's last moments. I now can accept that God pulled Chris home without any pain or fear. For that insight I will always be grateful to Dr. Mary C. Neal.

The verified events of countless other NDEs are available in books and online. I encourage you to take a trip to the other side through research. The subjects have all visited the place where my son now resides. So, it became important to me. And it's a place we are all going so it should be important to you, too. Besides, it's a lot nicer than that frat house in DeKalb Chris lived in. Even though the residents of that frat house, who lived there when he did, have become family to us.

Another phenomenon is Near-Death Awareness (NDA). According to PALLIPEDI (The Free Online Palliative Care Dictionary), near-death awareness can be defined as follows: "Near-death awareness (NDA) is a term to describe a dying person's experiences of the dying process and broadly refers to a variety of experiences such as end of life dreams or visions. Up to 50-60% of patients could experience some form of NDA prior to their death."

Several common experiences relating to NDA have been described and include:

- Communicating with or experiencing the presence of someone who is not alive.
- Preparing for travel or a change.
- Describing a place, they can see in another realm (i.e. heaven).
- Knowing when death will occur.

For the complete definition of NDA, along with more information on this in general, please see the Appendix.

Most third-party books that discuss NDEs usually include NDAs. The deeper you dig, the more familiar you will become. In layman's terms, when one is on death's doorstep, particularly if the dying process is in stages, they are visited by loved ones who have crossed over. In the past, most medical experts believed this was a hallucination brought on by the trauma of dying, medication, or deterioration of the faculties. Not anymore. Medical support staff are now educated in the NDA phenomenon. Consequently, medical staff who are witness to crossing over consider it commonplace and often part of the dying process.

The narrative that follows is an example of a deathbed vision story from *Visions at the Hour of Death*, by Stephan Wagner:

> The phenomenon of deathbed visions has been known for hundreds, even thousands of years. Yet it remains unexplained simply because what happens to us after death is still a mystery. By reading others' stories of visions before death, we may get a glimpse of what awaits us after this life.
>
> The following is a story with a very common theme. When we are approaching death's door our loved ones come to escort us home.

MOTHER'S DEATHBED VISION

My mother had been in and out of hospitals over the last year, near death at each admission. She was coherent and not delusional. She had congestive heart failure and lung and kidney cancer spread throughout her body. One morning in the hospital room, about 2 a.m. when all was quiet, my mother stared out the door of her room and into the hall that led to the nurse's station and the other patients' rooms.

"Momma, what do you see?" I asked.

"Don't you see them?" she said. "They walk the hall day and night. They are dead." She said this with quiet calmness.

The revelation of this statement might send fear into some, but my mother and I had seen spiritual visions many years prior, so this statement was not a shock for me to hear, or for her to see. This time, however, I did not see them.

Her surgeon said there was no point in treatment as cancer had spread throughout her body. He said she might have six months to live, at the most; maybe three months. I brought her home to die.

The night of her passing, she was restless and anxious. A few minutes before 8 p.m. she said, "I have to go. They're here. They're waiting for me." Her face glowed and the color returned to her pale face as she attempted to raise herself and stand up. Her last words were, "I have to go. It is beautiful!" And she then passed at 8 p.m.

I have not personally experienced a NDE or witnessed a NDA. But through four years of research I have been exposed to many books, presentations, and accounts by credible persons who have. So, I totally buy in. I believe it in my soul. I look at it like this: I have never seen the Great Pyramids of Egypt but enough of the world has seen them and reported back that I have no doubt they exist. And I believe that, too. In my soul.

CHAPTER FIVE:

THAT'S HOW THE LIGHT GETS IN

"There is a crack, a crack in everything, that's how the light gets in."
~Leonard Cohen

"A bruise on the leg is a hell of a long way from the heart… Candy Ass."
~Kurt Russell (playing Herb Brooks in *Miracle*)

The "A bruise on the leg…" is a quote from *Miracle*, the movie about the USA hockey team that won the gold medal in the 1980 Olympics. To get there they had to beat the previously unbeatable Russian Team.

The task wasn't for the faint of heart. And grief's like that; it's a messy business and whatever you have to do as a parent to get through the hour, day, year, the anniversary, the birthday… you do it.

This is an important message for parents. Winston Churchill once said, "If you're going through hell, keep going." That doesn't mean get over it, as in, "Isn't he over it yet? It's been five years." The answer is no. And I won't be over it until I cross and am reunited with my boy. But I do keep going. And I do want to emphasize this: grieving and surviving the physical loss of a child is a messy business. Get messy. At some point almost every day, I find myself letting go and crying. I don't go home or go back to bed (but if you have to do that, that's ok, too), but I stop doing what I was doing before my mini breakdown and cry, and feel, and hurt. And then I continue with my task of providing a living for my family and honoring my son.

So, here's my point (I have one, honest). I was raised in a family where both toughness and gentleness mattered. I have grown up in the company of men who suck it up when they get physically injured, or fatigued, but also allow their tenderness to show. Especially, or in the case of family, maybe even exclusively when it comes to family. It is very common for me to have to stop and take a quick moment during a presentation. That's ok, that's who I am. When I talk to the Ranch boys every March, we all begin composed and dry eyed. But it rarely ends that way. And if you've come this far with me on my journey—our journey—you know I'm not a candy ass. I've come a long way on this path. And this is who I am. And if someone judges how I conduct myself, I sincerely hope the door doesn't hit them in the arse as they leave my life. For my last lap around the track of life I want to surround myself with people like you. Who love, and grieve, and give, and keep going.

On pleasing others, I'd like to share this quote from Rumi: *"Half of Life is lost in charming others. The other half is lost in going through anxieties caused by others. Leave this play, you have played enough."*

I have rarely been constricted by the judgement of others. But certainly, once I had gone through the physical loss of my son, I have felt the desire to do only what I want to do. Or what I think (sometimes after prayer and meditation) is the right thing to do.

What I love about Helping Parents Heal and other such groups online and in person is that each and every member knows what I know. They know what we know. We can post things—events, thoughts, anniversaries. We can do that because we are all in the same boat. We aren't looking for someone to fix us. We aren't looking to get over it. And we aren't stuck. Our hearts are indeed broken, and will always be that way. But we function (sometimes not) and we share. We aren't looking for pity or sympathy. But it's where we can safely go for understanding. A burden shared is a burden halved. I personally feel I can drop the rock, because you know. If you're still reading this book, then you know.

One thing we have to do is to understand. People with totally good intentions sometimes speak from their ass because they don't know what else to do. It's akin to me telling an amputee, "I know how you feel." I have not lost a limb. Our departed kids want kindness from us. They expect kindness from us. In my case, I was given a gift of being Christopher's dad on this side of the veil for twenty-one years. I continue that role now, and we will be together again when I cross. When people tell me how sorry they are about Chris, I smile and say, "Thank you." I had the greatest job on the planet for twenty-one years. Through all the pain I've experienced over the last five years, I have had ten times that in joy. If given the choice I would make the same deal to be Chris's dad any day of the week and twice on Sunday. You needn't waste your pity on me, because by being Chris's dad I have experienced heaven on earth. And I know it.

APRIL 5, 2018

Hi Dad. It's not what you thought. These moments, time and me. Next to you and through you. Finish the book. It's already done, just put it on paper, put it together. I love those moments too. It's just different. I miss you and love you. I don't miss my old life really. Just some aspects. You know. I was a happy baby, but it was hard to be a kid. It's me Pop, just accept it. In and out, that's how it goes sometimes. But these moments connect us. Forever is in these moments. Don't be proprietary with the book. Let it out.

Affairs of the day have kept you in your world, that's all. We're still connected. Green Flash, remember? We never did see that did we? Looking for it now. That's me showing you.

*   I'm doing good work here. I'm helping Will. Keep up the love, I'll add guidance. When you start to doubt, remember the beach—Sarasota. You and me walking. You'll be able to see me. This is the next move. Some work to do though. But it will come. Feel me on your neck. That's me Pop. I love you too & miss you. You make it about me. You always did. A feather in the meditation. That's for you Pop, me to you. A gift Pal. I remember it all too Pop. The golf lesson. Driving the golf cart. Sleeping next to you in the hotel room. Casey is with me. Every day. She was waiting for me. She missed me. You did what you could Pop. I'm here and love you.*

Chris

Not a whole lot of explaining to do. Not really. When Chris was a kid—around age four or five—we stayed on Captiva Island, Florida for vacation a couple of years. We would spend a few days at Aunt Marcia's in Naples and then the rest of the week at a hotel or resort. On Captiva there was a restaurant called the Green Flash. We asked the waiter what 'green flash' meant. He told us about the phenomenon, and that our location was a prime spot for catching a glimpse of one. We never did see one and I completely forgot about the incident. But Chris didn't. He remembered.

Wikipedia describes the green flash like this:

The green flash are meteorological optical phenomena that sometimes occur transiently around the moment of sunset or sunrise. When the conditions are right, a distinct green spot is briefly visible above the upper rim of the Sun's disk; the green appearance usually lasts for no more than two seconds. Rarely, the green flash can resemble a green ray shooting up from the sunset or sunrise point.

Green flashes occur because the earth's atmosphere can cause the light from the Sun to separate, or refract, into different colors. Green flashes are a group of similar phenomena that stem from slightly different causes, and therefore, some types of green flashes are more common than others.

From now on, I'm going to start looking for the green flash. And when I see one, which I now know I will, I will know it's from Chris. See, that's the beauty of all this. Not only does Chris point out a memory we shared that allows me to return in my mind, in my memory, to a cherished time with my son, but it also helps to know that he feels the same about those memories. And talk about validation. I didn't remember the encounter until he brought it up and allowed me to revisit that moment. That pure, sweet moment we shared.

I also now know our Lab Casey is with Chris all the time. And I fully expect her to greet me with Chris when I take the step across.

(Flash forward to Lido Key, February 26, 2021. After dinner at a sidewalk café on St. Armand's Circle, Sally and I drove to Lido key to catch a sunset. And there as the sun dipped below the horizon… I saw it. I saw my first green flash. Thank you, Christopher.)

APRIL 11, 2018

Hi Dad,

I'm doing my things. But you aren't keeping me here. I am able to do both. Visiting you is important to me too. We stay connected all the way through Dad. Then you cross and we are still connected. It's a two-way street Pop. I love this time too. I'm not limited. You'll get it, but not quite yet. Just accept that you're not imposing. It fills my spirit. I'm still your son & always will be. I was always proud of you as a father. I still am. The outing, the anniversary, the pub crawl. My pals all love you. You're the man. Like a boss, remember? Just write it. It's me, not you. Good work at The Well. I was there. Most had a gift, some just wanted attention. I knew it too. I don't take on your sadness Dad. Just the love. It's ok. Finish the book by Father's Day, ok? A gift to me on your day. A gift to fathers on their day. Especially fathers who lost kids. Good plan, right? So get going Pop. Do that responsible thing you do. Like fixing Caroline's apartment, Will's school, and my grave. Too funny Pop. Gotta love that. You're a favorite up here too. Just like with my friends. Image and likeness. Deep, right? We're good Pop. I'm here, always will be. You're my dad and not a distraction & I love you. Get up and work on the book, I've got work too.

Love Ya,
Chris

It's funny that up to this point I was worried his spending time with me was taking him away from something more important on the other side. I'm over it. I don't know when I got over it, but I did. I bet a lot of parents struggle with this. Sometimes, we just have to get our arms around the fact that we can't get our arms around some things. He says, "like a boss." That memory again made me smile. On an early visit to the Ranch, I took over the dinner plans and included a friend or two and his buddy referred to my taking charge "like a boss." Chris smiled and I could tell he was proud of his old man. Sometimes, those little memories are enough to keep me going.

CHAPTER SIX:

You Just Gotta Drop the Rock

"It ain't what you don't know that gets you into trouble.
It's what you know for sure that just ain't so."
~Mark Twain

If you've come this far with me, you have most likely bought in. You've bought into the fact that whoever you loved who crossed is still with you. As Suzanne Giesemann, highly acclaimed author and medium tells us, they are "still right here." They are on the other side but accessible to you. And you are accessible to them. You share your experiences on websites for organizations like Helping Parents Heal and Grief 2 Growth. You can completely drop your guard. You can share your grief as well as your experience, strength, and hope.

When I'm at the grave, I often connect with other parents, most of whom have read *My Search...* and I can drop the rock. But what about outside those groups? At work? In the grocery store? So, now you are either trying to connect or have connected with someone you love who is on the other side of the veil. How do you handle this new-found knowledge? Look, you've been given a great gift. My sister Marcia called it the greatest gift. On her death bed, Marcia told me "Joey, you gave me the greatest gift. I read your book and I'm not afraid to die." This from a person who was and is a great source of love for me all of my life. Marcia loved me unconditionally, even when I wasn't so lovable. Marcia loved Christopher, unconditionally. And she would provide a great source of love to him throughout his life. I know they are together and I will get more into this throughout this book. But that one sentence from Marcia, that I could take away her fear of dying to this day, fills me with pride and gratitude.

On January 9, 2020, on my sixty-third birthday I visited Jill Nicole, an amazing medium located in the far west suburbs of Chicago. I will cover that reading in greater depths later, maybe in my next book, but she told me that my sister was with Chris. And she stated that Marcia told her I gave her "the greatest gift." Holy cow. My boy was buried on January 8, 2016, the day before my birthday. I have never made a big deal out of my birthday. But… this birthday gift from Marcia was a precious validation. What does that have to do with how I handle the muggles in my life?

Those muggles… In J.K. Rowling's *Harry Potter* series, a Muggle (/ˈmʌɡəl/) is a person who lacks any sort of magical ability and was not born in a magical family. In other words, regular folks who just don't get it.

Now, in my case… I don't care. I have been given this amazing gift of connection and I feel blessed and fortunate to have been given this. Also remember, I was born into a semi-dysfunctional, Irish-Catholic family. (One family friend who happened to be a psychologist once toasted, "McQuillens put the fun back in dysfunction.") We had ten kids, loads of friends, and a petting zoo of animals. Touch football games would spontaneously break out in the street. The parties ran late and tended to be loud. It was frankly terrific. It also gave me the security of being part of a tribe. We protected our own. Our own included generations of friends who had become family over the years. From my oldest brother Jerry's close friend Paul Hassett, to my dear pal Allen Conrad, to Debbie's best friend Colleen Hannah. Jerry and his friend Paul have both crossed but remained close all their lives. Allen and Colleen are both still both active members of the McQ clan, even after all these years (See? Fun back in dysfunction). Because of that strong family bond, I grew up not caring much what others thought. Especially about us. That lesson has served me well. I remember my first interview on the radio. The host asked me what I wanted to tell listeners who just didn't buy into all that jazz I was discussing. I told her to tell them to change the station. What I was given was a gift to carry a message I know is true, that I know is reality. It's a healing message full of hope, full of love. And if that's not for you, that's fine. Then tell your story walking.

I am contacted by parents who've been disappointed by friends and family who don't understand, much less support them on their journey. For the first year after Chris crossed over, Sally stopped going to the grocery store because people she knew would look away or change direction with their shopping cart. It was very hurtful and disappointing. She would also find herself in a discussion with a fellow mom who was prattling on about her kids (peers of Christopher) and their various upcoming life events—graduations, reunions, birthdays, and so on. They didn't realize their announcement would be a sharp needle in Sally's heart. But it was. Remember, Sally is a sweet, loving person.

I, on the other hand, was ok with people who turned away (it didn't happen as often to me). Maybe it's because I don't invite interaction when I'm on a mission at the grocery store. Or maybe it's because I don't really mind. I've got my reality. I've got my truth. If it's over someone's inability to understand, then that's their restriction. Not mine. I care deeply about my own. I care deeply about other parents who have lost children on this side. I care as well for those healers (there are many in my life) who want to help others. If you aren't in this category, well, I guess it's best said by Jack Nicholson as Colonel Nathan Jessup, "I'd rather you just said thank you… and went on your way."

But there are others. Thank God there are others. The friends and neighbors who have rallied. Friends who see you and smile. That look that says, "I want to help but I don't want to disturb you." I respond with a slight nod or a wink. I know they care.

I hope this helps. I hope my message is clear. There are legions of us who want to help you with your burden. Find out who those people are in your life and lean on them. Don't go where you may be disappointed. Listen to Bill Withers' words in his song…

> "Lean On Me"
> *Lean on me, when you're not strong*
> *And I'll be your friend*
> *I'll help you carry on*
> *For it won't be long*
> *'Til I'm gonna need*
> *Somebody to lean on*

From Colonel Nathan Jessup to Bill Withers. I sure do tend to run the gamut, don't I?

Saturday, April 14, 2018 was the third annual Chris McQ Pub Crawl held by his Northern Illinois University (aka NIU) pals. They booked a private room in a club in St. Charles, Illinois. The celebration was still on both of our minds at 3:00 a.m. the next morning. It was his birthday.

APRIL 15, 2018

Happy Birthday, Chris.

Thanks Dad, that was great. All my friends all having fun. I was all over the place. Momma was happy and Will was light and loved and loving. I'm working it on this side. On your side too. I'm not leaving you ever, (it's) just different. You don't need as much but I'm here.

Great to see you with all my friends. They all love you. You fit in with them. They are so comfortable around you. They know how much you love me, and they do too. Almost said as well. Funny, right? You always come through on my birthday but this one was special. Momma made me smile. You're a good guy Pops & a great dad. I would have been a great dad too. William will figure it out. He was at peace with our love yesterday. I'm here. Cassidy feels and sees me. She followed you into the office, my bedroom, because she always hung with me. My roommate. Especially when I was recovering from the fall. I love that dog. Casey is here and is with me all the time. Her choice. She'll be with me when you cross.

Good meditation. I'm with you in it Pop. My friends, Dad. Needed you to get to know them. In many ways they taught me another level of love & trust. So much love Pop. That's what matters. I'm proud of you Dad. Such a good dad. Loved hanging with you. Always easy. Thanks for that. You always got me and that always made me feel better. Feel more safe.

Listen to (the) meditation. I'm there behind the door. I'm there in the hotel room in Scottsdale. Thank Uncle Mike (Sawyer). That's me Pop. Feel it on the back of your neck. Chills, right? See my smile. That's how you made me feel & still do. I'm good with you Pop. Always was. When you would pick me up anywhere, I knew I could just let you take care of things. When you cross I'll

*take care of you. Trust in me now, I'm on it. You were more than
a dad, you were a friend. What a great combination. That's love
and faith Pop. Big deal... I'm good, I'm with you Pop. You did
good yesterday Pop. Made me proud. You always did.*

I love you
Chris

Interestingly, as I'm currently writing this book, I was clearing
off a shelf on my dresser. It's the shelf that holds a ceramic bowl
I keep my watch and bracelet in and a tray that holds good pens
(Mont Blancs). I was rifling through a few receipts from the post
office and throwing them out, and I came across a receipt from
April 14 for over $200. I didn't recognize the restaurant. There
were only three receipts on the shelf; two for postage and this
one. I brought the receipt into my office and Googled the name
of the restaurant. The Library, in St. Charles. Then the awareness hit, and I looked more closely at the date. It was April 14,
2018. It was the pub crawl. The receipt was two years old and
sitting on a shelf with two recent receipts. A shelf I use every day.
Hell, I am at it at least two times a day and here is this receipt. I
sat back and smiled. And thanked Chris for the connect. It was
his way of saying thanks for always being a part of his friends'
celebrations. Of making them feel important, because they are.
That was Chris's way. And that was part of our deal. My love
language. When I showed love and kindness to his friends it
deflected directly to him. It was an *I love you* directly from me.
Thanks for the acknowledgement, Chris.

APRIL 16, 2018 READING WITH SHARI ELMAN

On April 16, 2018, I had a reading with Shari Elman. She is a medium who I met at a spirit circle at The Well in Wilmette. It was a meeting place for presentations, group sessions, and spirit circles. The week before, I had attended a spirit circle and was struggling with some messages I was receiving. You see, we are all flawed creatures and our interpretations can be slightly off or just plain wrong. In this circle, I was getting messages from members of the group about letting go, etcetera. It sounded like they were telling me I was holding Chris back on the other side. This didn't wear well. One thing I was confident about was that I was incapable of holding my boy back on either side of the veil.

During this session that I was anxious to extricate myself from pronto, I caught the eye of a gal across the table slightly shaking her head no, side to side. It was clear she did not sign off on the group response. After the session, she handed me a card that let me know she was a medium. The next day or two, I called and scheduled a session, and boy was I glad I did.

Shari told me Chris was present and a very strong spirit. She told me I was carrying guilt and it was weighing on my spirit. She told me I should not have any regrets. I should write out all my regrets on paper, not reread them, and burn the document. She said Chris will be with me when I do that. She told me Chris isn't going anywhere and that there is really no such thing as time. In response to The Well meeting, Shari told me I wasn't holding Chris back, but rather my grief was holding me back. She told me that all souls have a circumference of three feet around us. Shari told me Chris is doing what he can from the other side and he is with me. He is now part of everything. Letting go is not letting go of him but rather letting go of guilt. Ok, so here is where it gets good... or really tough. She told me my guilt isn't about not being able to save him from the water, but rather about other things I could have done. This is what my guides are telling me I need to understand. They tell Shari that my journey is my journey and his journey is his journey. Chris is saying that and my guides (spirit guides) are saying that. He had a lot of sadness in his life and he is free of that. He had certain contracts to fulfill.

Chris said when I do things with his friends, he is always with us. I know he is always with me. My guides tell Shari I am searching for something, which is why I keep attending the sessions. It's fine, she says. She ends by telling me a lot of people just wear a physical body with a soul. I don't know what that means... I should probably have asked. This was the session where Shari told me Chris and I were twin flames. I discussed that earlier. But as soon as she said that I knew it was true. Even though at that time I only sort of knew what the term meant. Deep in my soul, I knew it was true. You see, that's it. The knowing versus believing.

That was a pretty cool session. I record these sessions on my cell phone and then transcribe them when I am preparing to enter them into this book. This session stood out. It was clear to both Shari and Chris that the previous circle had upset me. I wouldn't do anything to cause Chris any harm or slow his progress. They saw this and needed to get me back on the right track. They did. The good mediums give it to you straight. "He had a lot of sadness in his life." Damn, I didn't want to hear that. But it was true. I was compelled to meet with Shari. At the time I was feeling her reach out to me at the circle I had no idea she was a medium. But Chris knew. He also knew the little things had haunted me. Small missteps in parenting. Losing my temper. Choosing to do something instead of spending time with him. Those things continue to gnaw at my heart. And although I did a list not long after the reading, I need to do another one.

A comprehensive one I will take to his grave at night and burn. I doubt it will let me completely off the hook, but if you are anything like me, you really don't want to be.

CHAPTER SEVEN:

"BECAUSE THAT'S WHERE THE MONEY IS."
~Willie Sutton

Willie Sutton (infamous bank robber) reputedly replied to a reporter's inquiry as to why he robbed banks by saying, "Because that's where the money is."

People have often asked me, Why do you need to go to the grave?

I often go to the grave because that's where Chris is. Let's be clear. I know he doesn't live there. But I also know it's a *thin place* for me, and for others. That's where we meet. Our spirits move easily in that place. By now you know I stop by the grave a few times a week with a folding chair, often with my Lab, and always with a cigar. Why always the cigar? I'll explain in detail a bit later on in this chapter. First, I am *clairalience,* which means clear smelling. No kidding. More on this later, too. I can sometimes (not always) smell him when he's around. To me, it's the smell of an active teen boy, which he sure was, i.e. sweat. Knowing that smell can transcend the veil is comforting to me. I also know Chris associated cigar smoke with me. And finally, … I like cigars. You need to slow down and relax after you light a cigar. And that's just what I do in my folding Buffalo Bills chair next to his freshly polished gravestone. I take my time…

Because as I'm slowly starting to grasp, time really doesn't exist. It's just an illusion.

I also believe tobacco is an essential part of American Indian spiritual rituals. Check this out, verbatim as it appears on the Milwaukee Public Museum's website:

CEREMONIAL USE OF TOBACCO

Milwaukee Public Museum

In Woodland Indian rituals, ceremonies, and religious observances, tobacco is the unifying thread of communication between humans and the spiritual powers. The manidog (spirits) are said to be extremely fond of tobacco and that the only way they could get it was from the Indians, either by smoke from a pipe or by offerings of dry tobacco. According to tradition, the Indians received tobacco as a gift from Wenebojo who had taken it from a mountain giant and then given the seed to his brothers.

In almost all facets of their lives, Native people of the Great Lakes had reason to solicit the spirits for acts of kindness or to give thanks for past favors. Dry tobacco was placed at the base of a tree or shrub from which medicine was gathered, and a pinch was thrown in the water before each day of wild rice gathering to assure calm weather and a bountiful harvest. Before setting out in a canoe, a safe return was assured by offering tobacco on the water. On journeys or hunts, Indian men paused for a smoke and left a pinch of tobacco as an offering when they encountered certain features of the landscape, including waterfalls, misshapen trees, oddly shaped rocks, and lakes or islands said to harbor spirits. When storms approached, families protected themselves by placing a small amount of tobacco on a nearby rock or stump. Tobacco was placed at graves as an offering to the departed spirit. Requests to elders to relate oral traditions or other special knowledge were accompanied with a gift of tobacco.

Importance of Tobacco
Before all religious ceremonies, tobacco was offered to the spirits. The universal method of inviting people to feasts or notifying them of ceremonies was the delivery of a small amount of dry tobacco by a runner sent out for that purpose. When a shaman agreed to accept a client's case, he indicated it by taking the offered gift of tobacco.

(https://www.mpm.edu/plan-visit/educators/wirp/great-lakes-traditional-culture/tobacco)

YOU MEET THE NICEST PEOPLE AT THE CEMETERY.

That sounds crazy, doesn't it? But remember, I spend a lot of time involved in either speaking to Christopher, writing about encounters with the other side, or researching applicable metaphysical events. And when I say 'applicable,' I mean subjects that interest me. It's kind of a moving target. Yesterday, I swung by the grave with plenty of time to spare before a round of late-afternoon golf. I always have my folding chair and a ditty (carry) bag with cleaning, polishing, and pruning tools. The term "ditty bag" makes me smile even as I type it. I picked it up from my brother Billy (who is also on the other side) and I believe it followed him home from his stint in the Marine Corps, where he spent thirteen months in combat in Vietnam as a lieutenant. He was awarded the Purple Heart for injuries sustained in battle in the service of our country. Thank you, Billy.

Because we keep momentos left by friends on and around

the grave (along with a pink, plastic buffalo and green, metal cactus), the groundskeepers don't mow too close to the grave as to not disturb the loving collection. We are grateful to them for their consideration. However, every once in a while, I need to grab my weed whacker from the garage, throw it in the Jeep, and do some trimming around the stone. Of course, I have a system. I put all the momentos in a pocket in the ditty bag and then I trim around the grave. I have a big, old, squeeze water bottle (the hockey bottle I've kept since I hung up my skates last February). I have granite polish, scissors, a squeegee, and a golf towel. I trim, then I clean, polish, and replace the momentos back on the stone. It's a nice, comforting routine for me. Like straightening up a kid's bedroom. I am very proud of his grave. Even the goofy bison and cactus—maybe especially these items. I am proud that when his friends stop by, his headstone is always standing tall (and it always will be). It's my way of telling the visitor that Chris is, and always will be, loved and cared for by his parents. That may sound a bit silly, but I bet if you are reading this book, you get it. I love swinging by and seeing a rose, or a Landshark bottle placed on the stone. It confirms I'm not the only one who misses him.

The other people in the cemetery are like-minded, minus the pink buffalo. They come to visit someone they love. Pretty often, they visit their kids. There's Abigail's parents, who leave her Fritos in a basket; Robbie's mom, Maureen, and Maggie; Mike Crane's ex and Jimmy's mom. Chris and Jimmy were very close since junior high. Chris knew and very much liked Mike Crane and his grave is about twenty paces from Chris's. It's a loose community brought together by grief, love, and spirituality. So, you aren't likely to run into jagoffs (Chicago term) at Sacred Heart.

By the way, I have forgiven the owners for charging me to reintern Chris to one spot over to distance him from the couple to the south of him, mostly. I will occupy that space in time, but the site is perfect, and besides, I have a great story about the incident. Ask me sometime. Also, after five years, I have finally mastered the art of launching Chinese lanterns. After a long series of mis-launches, and a few minor prairie fires, I now know the secret. Email me and ask. I'll fill you in.

If you've read *My Search...* or heard me speak, now maybe you get it. You get why I go to Chris's grave. It's not out of duty or obligation. It's where I know I will feel his spirit. I can sit on my chair (after my clean-up detail). I can listen to a favorite song of his or mine, fire up a cigar, and look into the trees beyond the fence, and I can envision him walking through the clear American Airlines security wall, a duffle bag over his shoulder, and a big smile on his face. And I know I will see that sideways smile again when I cross over. Going to Chris's grave makes me feel whole.

When I was looking around the cemetery, something compelled me to look toward Mike Crane's grave. As I looked over, I caught a flash of scarlet and saw a cardinal swoop by. No surprise.

This chapter also brings me back to a story about Chris... I was working late and got a call at the dealership. Sally had taken the three kids to her brother Rick's lake house on Lake Beulah (yeah, that's the same lake). Her cousin Anne was over from France with her girls, and they were all planning a few days on the lake. Around 8:00 p.m., I got a call from Chris. "Dad, you gotta get me out of here. All these girls are driving me crazy." I asked him if he cleared it with his mom and he said it was all clear. I jumped in my truck and headed north. An hour and maybe forty-five minutes later, I pulled in the driveway and there was my boy, duffle bag in hand, waiting. He jumped in the truck and breathed a sigh of relief. "Let's go," he said. So, we did. I had just lit a fresh cigar and was of course listening to Jimmy Buffet. When we were clear of the house and headed for the highway, Chris asked, "Can I have one of those?" I only had a relatively strong cigar left, but of course, I said yes. He was about twelve so I didn't feel too guilty about allowing him this indulgence. Besides, he just spent the better part of a day immersed in enough estrogen to sink a battleship. He could use a little manning up if that was his choice.

We smoked and drove and listened to Jimmy Buffet. We talked a little bit and as usual on these occasions he completely let his guard down. It was him and me and it was perfect. Except for maybe that damn strong cigar. As we pulled into the driveway of our home, he opened the door and spit up a bit. I was concerned and asked about his well-being. But he said, "Dad it's fine, it was vomit of joy." Hmmm, ok I'll go along with that. Besides, we were together, just being. And it doesn't get any better than that.

MAY 4, 2018

Hi Pop,

We shared songs & we still do. For me, it's all vibrations. But I hear and feel every note, every word. We lived it out through music. I love that. See, you worried for nothing. I'm here. Great stuff with the book. My book, our book. Really proud of you. So glad I'm working on it with you. None of it's work, it's all love, and love and more love. Old Will is coming around. You are right about my Jeep. It will always be mine. It was so important to me. Not the pickup and not the Patriot, but the Wrangler and I were one. Weird huh? But we connect to things. Energy, it's all energy.

Thanks for the Chinese lantern right after my birthday. Loved my birthday, and loved my friends, and love all of you. That made me so proud that it was all about me. I didn't know that when I was on your side that I was so important to you all. But the love is so clear, so crystal clear. Get it?

Summer is coming and we can hang out at the grave. Feel me in the room now Dad. I'm all around you. Hugging you now. Shari E is right. You are not holding me back. You are my connection to your side, and I don't want to let go. And I don't have to, either. I can be all around. That's energy. That's the deal Dad, foot prints, energy prints. That's it, Pop. New levels are opening up to you. It's powerful Pop. I know you do Pop & I love you too. Blue is love, soft green is love. When you step over you will go "oh man, I get it."

Pure energy Pop. Don't limit yourself. You can come over here and come back. Work on it. Next project, right? The Source says hi. He is all love, she is all love. So am I, you too. Good job today. A new level Pop. Proud of you. Finish the book and be open. It's me driving the boat. Like in Disney, remember?

I love you
Chris

Well that's pretty cool. Chris talks about energy and footprints and me coming over to his side and back. That's astral travel and we will get there. He makes reference to driving the boat in Disney. When he was maybe five, we went to Disney World and he was picked to drive the jungle river boat in one of the park rides. There he was with his proud smile steering the boat with a big wooden boat wheel. The Steamboat Willie kind. Man, I had forgotten. But he didn't. That seems like yesterday. He also sends a shout-out from the Source. So, basically, God says Hi. I must be doing something right.

Since we just discussed clairalience at the start of this chapter, and since we're talking about connections and communicating, check out all the clairs. And who better than Rebecca Rosen to fill us in. The excerpt that follows is from Rosen's book, *Spirited: Connect to the Guides All Around You.* This excerpt also appears on Oprah.com. I think it fits well here, given the conversation we've been having so far in this book. See what you think after reading it.

INTUITION 101: DEVELOPING YOUR CLAIR SENSES

By Rebecca Rosen

Whether you refer to it as a gut reaction, instinct, foresight or a certain knowingness about events that haven't yet taken place, everyone has the gift of intuition. Are you listening to the signs and signals? Psychic medium Rebecca Rosen explains the five clair senses, what they are and how to identify and develop your strongest clair sense in order to open the door to powerful guidance that will help you create a meaningful and magical life.

Early on when I was developing my spiritual connection, I battled with tremendous self-doubt. It was hard for me to not compare my particular style of connecting with other mediums' experiences. It was clear to me that many mediums actually did "see" dead people or ghostlike apparitions. I wondered, "If I'm not seeing these ghosts standing next to the person I'm reading for, does that mean I'm not really connecting to spirit?" Meanwhile, I was, in fact, receiving profound validations or evidence from spirits to convince both the people I worked with and myself. There was a genuine connection being made.

As I started to explore the language of spirit and better understand how intuition works, I realized that my dominant way of receiving intuitive information was a more auditory experience rather than a visual one. The irony was that once I let go of my desire to "see," I started to recognize spirit energy as sparks of light, orbs and swirling wisps around the room. With time, I learned that while we have one or two dominant physical senses, we also have dominant intuitive senses and that we all connect with spirit in our own unique way. Our job is to figure out what way that is and then simply embrace it. And that's exactly what I'm going to help you to do.

Like radio waves, spiritual information is constantly being broadcast around us, so it's really just a matter of learning how to tune in to it. To interpret what spirit is broadcasting, you'll be using your five senses just like you do in your day-to-day life. And just as you may feel that some of your senses are more reliable than others for making everyday judgments, you have senses, or clairs, that are stronger for connecting with spirit.

The clair senses are types of psychic abilities that correspond with the five senses of seeing, hearing, feeling, smelling and tasting. When I tap into my intuition and spirit energy, my mind and body become flooded with mental impressions: thoughts, feelings, images, sounds, tastes and smells. To help you determine what your dominant clairs are, let me start by first explaining what they are and how our preferred senses shape our lives.

Clairvoyance means clear seeing.
This is when visions past, present and future flash through our mind's eye, or third eye, much like a daydream. Many of us are highly visual and able to understand an idea best when we see it written or sketched out as an image on a computer screen or on a canvas. Visual people often choose to be artists, builders, photographers, decorators, designers and so forth. If this sounds familiar, your clairvoyance is most likely a dominant sense.

Clairaudience means clear hearing.
This is when we hear words, sounds or music in our own mind's voice. On rare occasions, spirit may be able to create audible sound, though this takes a tremendous amount of focused energy. Some of us best retain and comprehend information when we hear it spoken aloud. Our natural talents tend to lie in our auditory faculties, often making us gifted musicians, singers, writers and public speakers. If this feels right to you, clairaudience may be a leading sense for you.

Clairsentience means clear feeling.
This entails feeling a person's or spirit's emotions or feeling another's physical pain. Many of us are clairsentient without consciously being aware of it. When we get a strong "gut" feeling, positive or negative, about someone we just met or when we get the "chills" for no apparent reason, we may be tuning into the emotional energy of a person or a spirit around us. When we are highly sensitive and are in tune with not only our own feelings, but also the feelings of others,

this makes us natural healers and caregivers. We often feel inspired to pursue careers as doctors, therapists, counselors, nannies and teachers. If this is you, clairsentience is at the top of your senses list.

Clairalience means clear smelling.
This is being able to smell odors that don't have any kind of physical source. Instances of this could include smelling the perfume or the cigarette smoke of a deceased relative, used as a sign of their presence around us. When our sense of smell is strong and distinct, we may find that certain smells connect us to past memories or we may be drawn to working as a florist, a wine taster or a perfume fragrance creator.

Clairgustance means clear tasting.
This is the ability to taste something that isn't actually there. This experience oftentimes comes from out of the blue when a deceased loved one is attempting to communicate a memory or association we have with a particular food or beverage that reminds us of them. If we have a heightened sense of taste, this would make us natural chefs, bakers or food critics.

Claircognizance means clear knowing.
This is when we have knowledge of people or events that we would not normally have knowledge about. Spirit impresses us with truths that simply pop into our minds from out of nowhere. An example of this would be a premonition: a forewarning of something that will happen in the future. Claircognizance requires tremendous faith because there's often no practical explanation for why we suddenly "know" something. Many philosophers, professors, doctors, scientists, religious and spiritual leaders and powerful sales and business

leaders tend to be highly intuitive and seem to just know the facts with a sense of certainty. If this is you, consider claircognizance as one of your dominant senses.

JUST MAYBE... GOD WAS RIGHT

I hear it, we hear it all the time. God has a plan. It was in his plan. Well, his plan really seems to suck sometimes. So, are you telling me that God's plan somehow included taking my boy and derailing our lives? I guess the answer is yes and no, and maybe. What is predestination? Webster defines it as: *the belief that everything that will happen has already been decided by God or fate and cannot be changed.*

I don't buy it. I buy into elements of it. But not that we are playing parts in a divine tragedy (sometimes comedy). Remember, my beliefs are based on my limited experiences. And maybe some experiences from another lifetime or two, or twenty. But we'll circle back to that. I do believe that sometimes God takes a hand—as in when Chris fell down the mineshaft, or when Chris flipped the pickup truck (both incidents were life-threatening). And sometimes he doesn't—as in when Chris took his leave from this physical world along with three pals in a canoe accident. I believe there are some cosmic rules we may not really be privy to.

In her book, *The Happy Medium*, Kim Russo tells us three's the charm. Or the reverse of that. She reports that after two NDEs, the next one usually results in an exit point. It's kind of like hall passes. There is a limit. So, if this is true then there can't be a pre-determined path we are set on. Which is very reassuring to me. Look, I did theatre in my youth. I know I surprised you with that one. Do I look like a guy who did theatre? But then again, do I look like a guy who would write about the metaphysical while burning a candle and sage? See what I'm getting at?

Book-by-its-cover stuff. But as much as I loved the theatre, as an actor you were living someone else's life on stage. Sure, you could bring in your own interpretations of the character, and yes, some of us took it too far...sorry about that. But basically, it's not your life on stage and you are limited by parameters. Get it? That's not what I signed up for here on earth school. By the way, I stole that term from the brilliant filmmaker Craig McMahon. I don't think we are wound up and set out on a predetermined path. For what purpose? God's amusement? You get it, right? But what about divine intervention or exit points—how do these fit in? Great question. The answer? I don't know. Really, I don't. But I do have some thoughts and beliefs that are subject to change.

EXIT POINTS AND SOUL CONTRACTS

I have touched on exit points a few times. Let's take a deeper look now. Here is an explanation by Guy Needler, author, energy healer, and Reiki Master: "Our souls have pre-planned not just one, but 3–5 exit points in every lifetime. It's the soul (not the ego) that gets to choose on the energetic level if and when to leave early."

Kim Russo, the author I mentioned previously, wrote about exit points in *The Happy Medium*: "It appears that all of us have 3–5 pre-planned times when we are meant to leave our body. These are called exit points."

Spiritual teacher Tanaaz Chubb defines a soul contract as follows:

"Before you entered this physical time and space your soul made an agreement.

Before you came into human form, your soul had specific purpose or destiny that it had agreed to fulfil. This destiny was written and is your Soul Contract. We all have Soul Contracts and essentially it is the list of lessons that we are meant to acquire in this life time in order to advance our soul to a higher level of consciousness."

(*Destiny, Fate and Soul Contracts* by Tanaaz Chub. For more info, visit the website:

https://foreverconscious.com/)

What struck a chord for me when reading (or listening) to Kim's book was that if someone has had two NDEs, the third one is always an exit point. This really lines up. Chris rolled a pickup truck, which was airborne, and later, he fell down a mineshaft where he was visited by an angel. But those times must not have been his time. But the third time is the one where he ran out of hall passes. According to Kim, this is just the deal.

And, to adjust a bit more to this discussion, here is how the Awake and Align blog author Sam Boomer defines a soul contract:

A soul contract is a non-physical agreement made on the soul level of your consciousness. You create them most often between members of your soul family and soul group before you incarnate into a new body, and they can detail all kinds of aspects about your life.

On Earth and other life-supporting planets, a soul contract is a binding agreement between one or more souls. It's an exchange of energy by way of fulfilling different roles and functions for one another. By doing so, you create shared learning experiences through scripted episodes of drama.

But these contracts aren't always positive. In fact, they're designed to create challenges, but ones that will help you grow on the soul level. The whole point of these agreements is that they'll provide some form of lesson that you can integrate and take forward with you.

And to that end, you can—and do—have more than just one soul contract when you come into a new life. Some will be new, while others will be holdovers from past lives you didn't complete through either your inability or because the circumstances weren't right.

The primary purpose of these contracts—as well as keeping order between souls—is personal accountability. They keep you honest on your journey and ensure you do what you say you will. They're meant to encourage your personal progress.

Because the fulfillment of soul contracts is ultimately how you raise your vibration, as the more wisdom you're able to amass, the more you'll be able to act from your highest intent.

(https://awakeandalign.com/soul-contracts/)

CHAPTER EIGHT:

SIX DEGREES OF BAT MCGRATH

We are all connected. I kind of believed that before, but like a lot of things in my life, it has turned into a knowing. In his book, *Answers About the Afterlife*, Bob Olson wrote that we are all one soul. He tells us to think about all our souls being a large body of water. An ocean, a lake. Each of our spirits are like waves, individual but always part of the lake. So, close your eyes and envision it. One body of water. Us, all of us, and God. And then envision the waves... that's you. Get it?

Yesterday, I was up early and wrote a little, and I did a little housekeeping (no, not that kind). I did some work on the upcoming Chris McQ V Annual Golf Outing, then I sent out some signed copies of *My Search...* to Andrew Anderson (for his clients) and one to Jeff Gould. Jeff was a counselor at the Ranch, and is a well-known expert on addiction in Dallas. But he travels the circuit speaking on addiction. It was important to Chris that Jeff and I become friends, so we did. He also just published a book titled, *A Life Concussed*. Pick it up. Jeff knows his stuff.

Over the last few days, I have been listening to one of my favorite singer-songwriters from the 1970s, Bat McGrath. Bat was a local guy from western New York, who was pretty big regionally. He was a large part of the Rochester music scene, but us Buffalonians claim him as one of our own. His music

touched my soul. He was a blue-collar balladeer and one hell
of a musician. He had two great (and I mean *great!*) solo albums
on Amherst Records. A regional label. I have listened to those
albums since my early twenties. He told our story, he told my
story. You can listen to and download these from YouTube. The
funny thing is, unknown to me, Chris became a fan. We would
drive together on one of my Tucson-to-Phoenix trips and old Bat
would get some air-time. Chris, it turned out, loved Bat's music.

I mentioned the upcoming Chris McQ V Annual Golf event.
We do it for charity, we do it for service, but mostly we do it for
ourselves. It keeps us connected. It keeps Chris at the forefront.
Part of the special outing is a concert on the patio after dinner. It's
a band we named Frat Dog, after the dog "Cooper," a Japanese
Chin, owned by one of Chris's frat brothers. Chris loved that
dog and kept a Twitter page for him, where Chris would bust
stones. He was and is a funny kid. Frat Dog is a group of pals
who happened to be accomplished musicians. We do one show
a year, at the outing.

Back in 2012, Chris was working as a Life Coach at the Ranch.
I thought I could combine a trip to hang with him with a little
service. I went to Brad Nye and Eric Simons, two of Frat Dog's
founding members, and floated the idea of doing a concert for
the Ranch boys. They loved it. We rounded out the group with
our west coast buddy Jimmy Cohn. The idea was to fly to Tucson,
where I had rented a house for the weekend, rehearse, dine on
BBQ steaks, and smoke cigars. The next day, we would drive to
Sierra Vista, an hour and a half south of Tucson, have a meeting
with all the boys, and then put on a brief show. You see, these
boys are engaged in recovery every day. They are surrounded
by desert and mountains. It is truly one of my favorite spots in
the world, yet it is a little desolate, and it is most certainly a thin
place. The veil doesn't get much thinner for Chris and me than

right there on that dusty ranch. So, I thought we could break up the monotony for the boys with a few stories and some music.

I rented a house through an internet vacation site and hoped for the best. We pulled the SUV packed with luggage and guitars into a big driveway in Tucson, and we all felt it. The universe was onboard. The house was an amazing space—maybe more like a compound—walled-in, with a gated patio and twinkling lights, a BBQ, hot tub, and waterfall. No kidding. I could almost envision a cosmic neon sign that read REHEARSE HERE! To a man, we knew we were on to something. We unpacked and did a shopping run for the steak dinner along with fine cigars that would be my compensation to the fellas (note "fellas" are the band mates and boys are Ranch kids... lots of male energy about). Aric, our lead guitarist, is also a fine lawyer who has helped me out of a jam more than once, including a minor legal jam involving Chris.

The plan was for Chris to come to the compound for a steak dinner, be the audience for the rehearsal, and hang out. He invited his buddy Sam DuPont, a fellow staff member and an In Balance Ranch alum, and a self-proclaimed Ranch kid. Sam had come to Chicago the year before and we went to dinner and he came over and hung out on the deck. He was regaling the family with stories of he and Chris. We couldn't get enough. We sat up until the wee hours. Sam brought his guitar to the cookout rehearsal and played some of his own songs. And I mean *his own*, written and performed by him. He was brilliant. We sat around the table in awe. He was a truly masterful troubadour and storyteller. He was immediately drafted as our opening act. My goodness, that was an evening. We did an impromptu rehearsal, and we were greeted with applause by the women who owned the house and lived on the top of the duplex. We knew we were in good form. Good enough for fifty bored, homesick Ranch boys at least.

I think back to that night with both comfort and heartbreak. As you know, it happens like that. I'm sitting in a compound in the desert with three of my best friends, Sam DuPont who would end up being like family to the McQs, and my sweet boy Christopher. Even then something stirred in my soul, and I knew this was something special.

The next day, we packed the SUV with guitars and cigars (now there's a country song!), as Brad would say. I was driving and Brad was copilot. Brad had an amazing career in music. He had a band called Dick Holiday and the Bamboo Gang. They were backed by Miller Genuine Draft and hit every big college campus in the country. He is a brilliant musician and a better friend. As we headed south, I played some music we would all dig. Crosby, Stills & Nash, Joni Mitchell, and a little Buffett. I picked out a song by Bat McGrath. I was introduced to him when I was Chris's age (then) and he's always been high on my list of favorites. His songs were like us—stories about blue-collar guys and their joys and struggles. I played one of his songs called "Blue Eagle" from his album, *At the Blue Eagle*. It's a tune about a guy who is sitting at a redneck bar having a few beers and ends up on the backroom pay phone (remember those?), calling an old love. *"Ordered one for the road and what do you know I end up crying on the backroom phone."* Dude, who hasn't done that? As we listened and I sang along, Brad asked who we were listening to, and I told him it was Bat McGrath. He said when he was with Van Halen on tour, the head of security was a guy with the same name.

I remember reading an article a number of years back about a time in Bat's career when he had given up music and worked on tour with a number of bands as security. By the way, Bat was a martial arts bad ass. The article recalled when a fan saw him in his current role and asked what the heck he was doing. "You're Bat McGrath for gosh sake!" He finished that tour and returned to writing and performing which he did until the end of his life. Six degrees—Brad, me, Chris, and Bat.

When we got to the Ranch, they had a cookout for us and Brad gave a lead to the boys with stories of Van Halen, Hall & Oats, and The Troubadour in LA. The boys were enthralled. When Betsy, Patrick's wife and co-owner/operator of the Ranch asked if I had anything to add, I checked my repertoire of stories and declined. You can't add anything to a good Brad tale. We had set up on a stage overlooking the desert and the setting sun. It was amazing. When Brad broke into the Tim McGraw song, "Live like you were dying," I caught sight of Patrick Barrasso, and noticed him physically pull back. I saw how absolutely moved he was. After the show, I approached him and asked about his reaction. He told me that the Ranch was founded to help heal boys who suffered from addiction. It had always been his dream. His longtime friend helped him create In Balance Ranch. When diagnosed with cancer, that friend embraced life to the fullest, despite his diagnosis and eminent death. That song had become his theme song. That song has been the song that is the glue for every Frat Dog performance. And it's always dedicated to Patrick.

By the way, a few years after Chris drowned, we attended a presentation by the world-famous medium Rebecca Rosen. We were in the middle of an audience of maybe 150 people. About halfway through the event she approached our section and asked who had lost a son in a canoe accident, who was twenty or twenty-one. She said we have a connection to country music. Sally and I both stood up. She said he is sending me a song, "Live Like You Were Dying." She also asked me who was the dog with the name Cooper? You just can't make this stuff up. Now, do you see what I'm saying? Six degrees. Bat McGrath, Me, Brad, Patrick, Cooper, and of course, Chris. We are all connected. You just have to look closely, with loving eyes.

Just the other day I was surfing the net and saw that Bat had died last fall. Something stirred and something hurt a little. But maybe Chris will sit in on a jam session on their side. The song, "Blue Eagle" goes on the Frat Dog play list this year. Chris, when you see Bat, tell him your dad said thanks.

CHAPTER NINE:

CROSSING THE BRIDGE

MAY 18, 2018

Hi Dad,

You've been busy with the book and that's great. Almost done. But we are always together. Editing, speaking, meditating. Isaac's here, he's safe. Still in process. But pain is over for him. Poor kid. Like husking corn, shedding the pain. It will be fine. Tell Cathy he's ok and he loves her. It's the same pain and it's a relief to know the day is done. The work on your side is over.

Your dad is here. The story brought him forward. He's been in the background supporting me. I love your dad, he's so sweet. Boy, does he love you. I love the lilies. You buy them but the idea is from me. Allen, Grammy, Momma. They are from me. Dude, the tattoo is awesome. I fixed it the first night, so it was perfect for you. So proud of you Pop.

Chills on the neck Pop, that's me Dad. We are doing this. Crossing the bridge to be together. Just the way I like it. I miss you too Pop. Let's meet at the grave tomorrow morning. This is a killer meditation piece. It makes a difference. It clears the air waves. Opens the portals of vibration. I love our book. No one who reads it won't be affected, won't be changed. The purity is the magic. It's the mojo Dad. It's us together that really makes me happy. Raise your consciousness & your energy. It's starting to get good Pop. So, hold on. We're in for a ride you and I. Always up for an adventure together, right Dad? Visit Marcia and get to the gulf. I'll be there. Heck I'll travel to the gulf with you. I helped you land on the ice last Sunday. A little rocky, rough landing but nothing broken. The angels did that for me in Arizona. A few broken bones but I came back to you. For a while at least. Loved the hospital. That locked us down forever Pop, forever Dad. Hard to explain energy, so don't worry about it. Just think of me as me.

Love you Pop
So very proud of you.
2 weeks no more.
Love you
Chris

Wow… just friggin' wow. Chris talks about the closeness we share when we are working on any aspect of the book. It brings our spirit into one circle. One of the reasons I'm writing this book is to self-ishly keep that connection strong. And also, because Chris told me to. And Chris and I are helping others to boot. So, there you go.

Chris tells me, "Isaac is here. He's safe. He is still in process." Let me explain. Isaac was a young man Chris grew up with. They lived a few doors down. As small boys they were inseparable. The parents divorced and then the family moved. But the boys had already moved on to different friend groups and we didn't see much of Isaac, after the early years. Cathy and Sally have remained close. And they share a bond. A sisterhood of women who worried constantly about their eldest boys. They had good reason… or not.

On May 15, 2018, a few days before this visit with Chris, Isaac died of an overdose. Man, that hit me. But so much more important was how heartbreaking it was for our friend Cathy. She carried the burden of his pain. His addiction. And although I loved both Cathy and Isaac, the world had distracted me. I am not arrogant enough to think I could have interrupted his destiny. But I wasn't even aware of his struggles. I had my own struggles with Christopher and career changes and so many other excuses. What was it the Ghost in *A Christmas Carol* said? I believe these were his words: "Mankind was my business. The common welfare was my business; charity, mercy, forbearance, and benevolence, were all my business. The dealings of my trade were but a drop of water in the comprehensive ocean of my business!"

"ON CHILDREN," A POEM BY KAHLIL GIBRAN

Your children are not your children.
They are sons and daughters of Life's longing for itself.
They come through you but not from you.
And though they are with you yet they belong not to you.
You may give them your love but not your thoughts,
For they have their own thoughts.
You may house their bodies but not their souls,
For their souls dwell in the house of tomorrow, which you cannot visit,
not even in your dreams.
You may strive to be like them, but seek not to make them like you.
For life goes not backward nor tarries with yesterday.
You are the bows from which your children as living arrows are sent forth.
The archer sees the make upon the path of the infinite, and He bends you
with His might that His arrows may go swift and far.
Let your bending in the archer's hand be for gladness.
For even as He loves the arrow that flies,
so He also loves the bow that is stable.

That's a lovely passage. That's what I thought before Chris drowned. And then and only then did I understand it. Really understand it.

Isaac had crossed over and all we could do now was attend the service and at Cathy's request, provide a piper to play the bagpipes. It was the least we could do. It did make me smile as I wondered how many Jewish Temples had been visited by a piper in full regalia while piping "Danny Boy." But that's what Cathy wanted. And that's what she got. It was while chatting with the piper that he told me the old Celts believe the pipes are the only instrument that can be heard on both sides of the veil. I don't know if it's true… I know music, at least in the form of vibration, plays a key part in our communication. But it got me thinking, and feeling, and it interrupted my crying for a few minutes. I cried for Cathy, and Erwin, and me, and Sally. But mostly I cried because the floodgates had opened, and I just couldn't stop. That's the way it goes sometimes.

In his May 18 visit, Chris also talks about the lilies. They always seen to pop up when looking for that right gift to send. I sent one to my best friend Allen on the anniversary of his wife Debbie's crossing. We met in September of 1971, the first day of School at Bishop Timon High School in South Buffalo. He has been my closest friend ever since. He informed me that the lily was in his office, and it brought a smile to his face when he looked on it. Debbie loved lilies. I didn't know that, but Chris did. And he was sure to take credit for the choice. He told me he loved my cardinal tattoo, and he made sure it healed correctly. Despite my lack of care, including submerging myself in the hot tub too early.

A few days later, I awoke early, around 1:00 a.m. I killed time. I watched some TV and took a dip in the hot tub. As it approached 3:00 a.m., I thought it might be time for a visit with Chris. While I got out of bed, I received a message: "Maybe it's time to write today." So, maybe it was. I turned on my computer, Facebook flashed on, and I saw a message from Suzanne Giesemann's spirit guide, Sanaya. When the guide of a retired assistant to the Joint Chief of Staff sends a message, one should pay attention. Suzanne, a retired US Navy Commander, has also become a world-famous medium and best-selling author after the death of her stepdaughter. When spirit decides to put you on a path, you need to embrace it. Or should I say, I need to embrace it. You need to do whatever you need to do.

Sanaya says: Do not be in such a hurry to "get there." Yes, "Enjoy the journey." It is most excellent advice. You are in a human suit for a reason. The experiences, the learning that results, and most of all, the connections, are why you decided to incarnate. If you had all the answers and were the perfect expression of the love of the Source, where is the contrast that allows you to celebrate those moments of awakening, of connection, of joy? Smell the flowers, drink the coffee, love with all your heart. Yes, remember who you really are, beautiful soul, as you do so, and then hold that Awareness in the heart as you play cards and walk on the beach and fix the car and mow the grass. It is all for the Joy of it, even the challenging times, for Love is ever-present. You are so very loved. It can be no other way.

This is sage advice. I was feeling like a slacker because I haven't been pounding out this book. I've been very busy with work (my other job) and golf, and family. And to be very honest, I'm a little afraid to finish this book. I am well over halfway through and it's my connection. My lifeline to my boy. The connection did not disappear or even lessen after *My Search...*, yet I still have that nagging fear. But writing is so important and so is finishing. One day, thank God (literally), but not today.

ON MAY 31, 2018, WE VISITED @ 3:40 A.M.

Hi Dad,

I was with you yesterday. That was a nice thing. Andrew saw me but I was holding back a little. He needed to heal and not focus on me. But he saw me, and you feel me. I look the same Pop, but this is my call. You'll see. Just like at the airport Pop. So happy to see you. So happy to be back. Home was with you, you'll be with me soon, and we'll be home. I can't wait to show it to you. You'll go nuts. It's so great. So free, so warm. It's completed for me when you join me. Like the walk at the retreat. Once around Pop. One more walk that doesn't end. I'm with you Pop. Don't cry, I'm right next to you. You have to feel me. In the same space as you, right arm over left. Remember.

I miss you more than anyone Pop. Miss you all. Momma, the kids and Mish. It's like I'm knocking on the window. Eventually they will let me in. I leave a trace like a scent or a streak and they will see and feel me someday. Momma knows. Good job Pop. Good job on the book. I really was an inspiration all the way so you could get behind it. You're my dad. So grateful for that. That will never change. I trust you Dad. Let others rest. Go see Marcia, get that done.

Big hug-Big smile-Big love.
I'm going back home. See you later.
Love
Chris

p.s. the rainbow yesterday was from me. Notice the green like I describe. A gift for doing a nice thing.

C

Well, that's friggin' amazing. One of the challenges of writing this book from notes taken a couple of years ago is that the relevance of some events eludes me. Chris mentions I did a nice thing, and he didn't want to spiritually impose on Andrew. Then it dawned on me that Andrew had a hip replacement and I had visited him that day at a rehab facility not far from his home. I remember it like it was yesterday. I drove out in a torrential storm. I brought him some Greek chicken. No one likes institutional food, right? The visit went well, and I felt we (Chris and I) did a nice thing.

I love Chris's message about the walk at the retreat, a treatment facility in Wayzata, Minnesota. I remember this walk like it was yesterday, and the grounds appear to me sometimes in meditations. I love how he talks about spiritually calling on family and friends. *"Miss you all. Momma, the kids and Mish. It's like I'm knocking on the window. Eventually they will let me in."*

Chris talks about the airport. When sitting at the grave, in my mind I often envision how he looked when he came through the glass security wall at O'Hare. He would walk to the glass exit with a sweet sideways smile and a duffle bag slung over his shoulder. As soon as I caught sight of him nothing in the world mattered. I guess some things remain the same on either side of the veil.

Chris talks about heaven. How I will go nuts when I join him. When I, too am home with him. And he talks about the rainbow. Halfway home from the visit with Andrew the rain ceased. It was replaced with the biggest, brightest rainbow I had ever seen. The one color that stood out was the green. I had truly never seen anything like it. Chris tells me that was my reward for doing a nice thing. I'll take it, believe me. But knowing Chris was proud of me and was with me was more than enough thanks for this dad.

TAKEN HOSTAGE BY A MEMORY

I was loading something in the back of my Jeep today. It could have been golf clubs, or it could have been my fourteen-year-old yellow Lab Cassidy. Both can often be found in the back of my truck. I have to lift my dog in and out now. Which isn't an easy task for either of us. Just another sign we are both getting old. As I did this, I noticed behind me a young, red-headed boy walking down my street with the carefree gait of a four-year-old; the walk of a soul, completely free of responsibility or worry. My God, for just a second my mind rolled back nineteen years and I thought fondly of Trevor. For just a second, a brief second, I thought it was Trevor. But reality and the present stepped in and I did stop myself before I looked behind Trevor for his pal and childhood companion, Chris. My boy Chris. Back in those carefree summer days they were never far from each other. Exploring the neighborhood, climbing trees, riding bikes, and one time using the electric garage door like an amusement park ride. But of course, it wasn't Trevor. Trevor has since graduated both high school—where he was a member of the State of Illinois championship hockey team—and college. I'm certain he graduated from college, I just can't recall which school. I do know he is working in the financial world in Chicago, and living with pals in the city. Updates from his dad make me smile. I loved that kid. Although a year younger than my Chris, he was fearless. Chris removed the training wheels from his bike because Trevor had done so. And so, it went. Trevor came from a wonderful family who moved next-door when Chris was four or five. His dad Scott and I remain friends to this day and Scott attends the Chris McQ Annual Golf Outing. I wonder if Trevor golfs? Wouldn't that be something if he joined his dad next year?

Once again, I was taken hostage by nostalgia. Back to those years in the late 1990s. I wish I knew how precious those years were. Hell, how precious those minutes were. Even writing this I have a stirring in my soul, in my whole being. Because Chris is inspiring this. He wants you to embrace the memory of those carefree days as parents watching your children navigate their world freely. And then I want you to embrace your spouse if lucky enough to still have one. Take a victory lap. Because you provided that for your child. You did that…nice going. Now here's the kicker: that's exactly how they feel now. Free. Free and unencumbered by fear, guilt, or results.

I had no idea where this chapter was supposed to go. But when I saw that kid, I grabbed a note pad I carry in my Jeep and wrote *Trevor* on a page. This morning, I was pushed to wake up and start writing. But not about the sadness. And not even about the life events we are cheated out of. I won't see Chris graduating from college, or walking down the aisle. I don't get to hear the words 'Grampa' from what would be the beautiful offspring of my boy. And that is truly painful. And I know you feel this pain also. But only now, I mean right now, I have a glimpse of the freedom of spirit that is his reality. He feels as free as a four-year-old boy in summer, hanging with his beloved best pal. And I now, and I mean right now know, that I, too will be given that gift when I am guided across the veil by my boy, Chris. There will be a lot of joy and sorrow, grief and love between now and then. But what a payoff, what a jackpot when I do cross over. I hope this helps you over the hump when you have your own Trevor moment. This path we are given to walk sure isn't an easy one.

When I read this to Sally, having to stop a few times to compose myself, she asked me, "Are you ok?" "No," I said, "but I will be."

CHAPTER TEN:
_____

EIGHT YEARS

My dad, whose nickname at work was Iron Joe, worked on the railroad for forty years. He was one of those amazing guys who you don't know is amazing until you've had your share of life experiences. As in, "taken your turn in the barrel." He had a very limited education, leaving school in fourth grade to help provide for his family after his own dad died. He would regale me with stories of those old jobs. Not complaining, never complaining, just telling. He drove a horse-drawn wagon delivering baked goods for Lang's Bakery as a kid. He would talk fondly of how his horse would know the route and abruptly stop to awaken the young delivery driver who was often asleep atop the wagon. Damn, I wish I remembered the horse's name.

I do, however, remember the name of his beloved German Shephard: Pal. See Dad, I was paying attention. I would ask my siblings about the horse, but most of them are on the other side, with Dad. The crazy thing is that for such a tough guy, we never ended a conversation in person or on the phone without saying, "I love you." He did love me. He truly did and I was secure in the knowledge that I was loved whenever I talked to him. My dad was not a sophisticated guy, and his lessons were simple. One being, "Do as I say, not as I do." He would recite a poem about the afterlife to me (us) as a lesson.

"We come into this world, all naked and bare. We go through this world with worry and care. We go out of this world to who knows where, but if we are goodfellows here, we will be thoroughbreds there."

Holy smoke… What an amazing life lesson to follow. Which I didn't, of course. I didn't even think of where we would go next. Or if someone was keeping score and thus bestowing thoroughbred status on some of us. But now, after Christopher's crossing and me approaching age sixty-five, this lesson is pure wisdom. I have seen many mediums. I mean amazing, world-class mediums, all who have seen Christopher and many who have seen my dad behind my boy in spirit. One medium told me my dad knows I need the focus to be on Chris, but my dad wanted me to know he was taking care of Chris.

My very first encounter with a medium was when I was going through a very heavy stretch of my life professionally. I was reckless and laid it all on the line, and it was teetering. This is what I mean about time in the barrel. I think I sought out this medium/angel expert as a gateway to some emotional peace. I was spinning. But the truth revealed itself a good sixteen years later. Anyway, I had this session that was not all that moving. Until the end. You see, I wasn't really looking to connect. There was no urgency. The spirit world responded in kind. But the Source knows what He's doing. And just as the session was about to expire, the medium, Nancine, told me my dad was present.

I sat up straight and started to hang on every word. She said he's showing her a caboose and telling me "railroad." She had no idea what that meant. She was merely delivering the mail. But we were a railroad family. Like every boy in the family, I worked during college and after on the railroad. I would go with my dad to his work on the railroad as a kid and often spend the night. The sounds of the railcars banging into each other was soothing music to sleep by. There was actually an occasional road trip in a caboose, later on when I worked with my dad. Holy cow. That message was just like my dad; simple, clear, concise. I came away knowing my dad who had crossed over thirteen or so years before was just telling me he was somewhere. Somewhere accessible. Sixteen years later, that message came surging back. Like a wave engulfing my whole being, when my Christopher drowned. If Iron Joe is somewhere accessible, I thought, then Chris must be with him. He's not gone, not really. Thanks Dad, and thanks Nancine. That memory from so long ago jumpstarted my search to find my boy.

Another story about my dad from just around the same time is taking my attention. I remember praying (albeit a fox hole prayer) because of business. I got on my knees and asked my dad for strength. He raised ten kids working double shifts on the railroad, and here I was melting. The following morning, I walked into my bathroom and saw a UTU (United Transportation Union) lapel pin encased in cellophane next to my basin. You see, not only did my dad have the most seniority in the region, but he was also the local chairman for the union. He represented his men. We actually had a separate union phone inside a cupboard attached to the inside of the door. We called it the Bat Phone. We were mischievous kids but even we never messed with that phone. That pin was there, on my sink. How could a union pin from the seventies, when I worked on the railroad, have followed me to another state some twenty-five years later? Riddle me that, Batman. I asked Sally and she knew nothing about it. I was starting to get the picture. My dad was around, and his namesake should start manning up.

And just in case this seems a bit out there for you, below is a picture of the pin which I keep in my jewelry box. Just this minute I added it to a box holding Chris's beloved AKL Fraternity pin.

I keep it on my desk and look at it often when I'm writing. I will bring the UTU pin to my next medium session to see if it helps to connect with my dad.

Dad's UTU lapel pin.

But back to the title of this chapter, "Eight Years." My dad was born July 13, 1917 and crossed over on January 25, 1988. Dad retired from the railroad in 1980. He had eight years to enjoy a lifetime of endless work. Eight friggin' years. Mom and Dad bought a modest trailer with a patio in a park in Pompano, Florida. It was really, really nice. My Uncle Bill and his wife Bea lived in the same park as did other railroad retirees. They golfed, had cocktails on the patio, and played cards. My Dad was in heaven (before actually being in heaven). Eight years is so short. I don't want to wait to be able to cash in and relax for eight years. I want to start now. You should start now.

I'm not talking about retiring. I could never retire. I'm talking about wearing life like a loose garment. By stopping and smelling the roses. Heck, I even put up a bird feeder and find great joy in watching the birds come to feed, especially the cardinals. It's a small step, but it's a step. Who would have thought?

Back to the book...

A little follow-up. I took my own sage advice. I spent the month of February and most of March in Naples, Florida at Marcia's house. Aunt Marcia's house. Technically, it's Marcia's two wonderful kids' Colleen and Norm's second home. This place is full of fond, loving memories and being here is as close to heaven as I've gotten. Both my kids have joined me at separate times, and Sally will join me in Siesta Key (a thin place of mine for the week). Although I continue to work, those burdens seem lighter. And writing Chris's story, while sitting on Marcia's lanai, seems natural. This is the only other place I've written a word of either book outside of my office. The office that was Chris's bedroom. And it feels so right.

ON JUNE 11, 2018, WE HAD A SESSION.

I'm glad you're done, but we've got a lot to do together. It's not over. The connection will never end. The energy is going to flow in and out. It's there it's just in a different form. Hard to explain. I'm not bailing on you Pop. I'm not your guide but I will always guide you. Our connection is now like a light switch. Just click it on Pop and I'm there. I'm an advanced spirit now. Still look the same to you & just slightly different to mediums. But always the same kid, always your boy. Feel that Pop, like a flush head to toe. That's me. That's spirit. The house in Florida, Marcia's home held my young spirit running around. Feeling love. A little bittersweet Pop, even for me. We feel that way. Saying goodbye, like when I took you to the airport in St. Paul. I was lonely when you left because I loved you so much and I was confused. You did a good job Dad. Feel me Pop. Now you know. You can still see Andrew, but you know I'm with you. Jeez Pop, you gotta know that I'm not leaving you ever. Marcia is already starting to transition. That was my focus. I know you are ok. She's scared, you won't be Dad. It will be like Crystal Beach when you get here. Plus, your mom and dad, Uncle Bill, Billy, Bobby and Dianne, everybody. Pat and Kerry are here together. Lots of love there—more than you know. Pat knows you're sorry about Evan. She forgives and loves you. You are her baby brother. Everybody loves you. Kind of like how everybody loves me. I get it now. We hang out and come and go. But they are all here for me, and each other. It's really comforting & nice.

Good Job Pop.
I'll help you with phase 2 of the book.
Love you Dad
Chris

I am transcribing this from a year and a half ago, and I'm amazed. I wrote this down in my own hand and yet the messages awe me. How could one visit cover and clear up so much? Chris makes reference to me being done. What he means is that he wanted me to finish the first draft of the book (manuscript) before Father's Day. And we came in ahead of time. And I mean we. He reassures me that the end of the book doesn't mean the end of our connection, or the end of our work together. Far from it, as it turns out. He tells me our connection is now instantaneous.

Like a light switch. He also tells me something that I will hear from my medium friend Andrew Anderson later that Chris looks a little different.

I did some editing of the book at my sister Marcia's house in Naples, Florida. She will join her siblings, parents, and beloved Godson Chris in early 2019. Chris was there when his Aunt Marcia crossed. I have felt him there while visiting Marcia who was pretty much home-bound with cancer. Chris let me know she was already transitioning. He also let me know what heaven is like—that it's pretty much a family affair, and that surely works for me. He gives me a message that Pat forgives me for an incident that occurred a number of years ago involving Pat and her grandson Evan. I had good intentions but made a poor decision. I've regretted it for years and although I've tried, I still somehow need to make amends to Evan, especially now that Pat has forgiven me.

Chris tells me he will help with phase two of the book. Editing and publishing and all that it involves. He did obviously because this is Book Two, get it?

ON JUNE 13, 2018, I HAD A VISION VISIT. HERE IS WHAT I WROTE RIGHT AFTER IT OCCURRED:

I miss you, Chris. I woke up to you next to my bed, after thinking I hadn't seen you in a while. You stood to the left & I actually saw you. First vision. I want to get closer. See more. You didn't say anything. Just looked at me and it was you. The moment between sleep & wake. Thanks for that.

I love you
Dad

CHAPTER ELEVEN:

THE LEADER OF THE BAND

One of the greatest lessons Dad ever taught me was "family first." He was all about family. He taught us to celebrate as a family, to circle the wagons, and to love each other. That's what counted. And the family friends over the years just became part of the circle. The inner circle. You know who you are. Every year except this year (COVID) we would join together as a family in Crystal Beach, Ontario for a week of family and love. And I know Dad always watches us from above with satisfaction. You taught us well, Dad. I have tried to raise my three wonderful kids with the same commitment to family. And it took.

It was Father's Day and I was on my deck with my dog drinking coffee. I wanted to run over to Sacred Heart Cemetery to visit Chris. I looked at my Lab and asked her if she wanted to visit Chris. Her ears perked up in anticipation of an outing. As I walked toward the garage, I began to get teary thinking about my son. Just then a small, red cardinal flew up and landed on a wooden fence post to my left. He remained still for a short time, then flew in a circle, and then flew away. That was it—that was my Father's Day gift from Chris, and I will cherish it forever.

Thanks, buddy!

"TRYING TO REASON WITH HURRICANE SEASON"

"Trying to Reason with Hurricane Season" is the name of a Jimmy Buffett song. It's a good song, and it's a great title. In six words, it describes what we go through. What we go through as parents who've lost kids, what anyone whose loved one has taken the step across to the other side goes through. I'm not sure how you did it. Hell, I have no idea how I did it. One moment, we are on a people carrier of life going forward (like at the airport). And the next, we have this safe dropped on us. We are given a time to grieve and then we are expected to step back on the people carrier. But it's not that easy. It's like doing a crossword puzzle in fifty-mile-an-hour winds. Everything seems almost impossible to do, and does it really matter? I know Sally felt that way. A trip to the market took on traumatic aspects. She felt she was on display as that mom who lost a kid. Yet reality had to be dealt with. The decisions about the kids' schooling, housing, and the future couldn't be put on a back burner because I wasn't up to the task. Here is a line from the poem "Richard Cory," by Edwin Arlington Robinson: *"So on we worked, and waited for the light."*

And that was it. On we walked, and on we worked. We did this with a piece of our heart across the veil. On the other side. I was fortunate. My boy came through to me early. I was able to shift my life and focus a good part of it where he was now. But I had to navigate that while staying present for my other two kids who were wrestling their own gorilla. A lot of that first year was a fog. I just kept walking down the path, hoping my decisions were more right than wrong. The last thing I wanted was to create more regrets. But to be honest, I didn't even think about it. Looking back now it's clear to me that Chris was helping guide me. He told me he wasn't my spirit guide but acted as one. I now see his handiwork in everything that year. Family decisions, work decisions, and decisions about our book. Decisions about the path my life was now taking. I'm proud of myself for surviving that first year. I also know I did some really good things to enhance my spiritual development. I didn't sit back. I couldn't sit back because I was pushed. And I know there is someone guiding you, pushing you if you just open up to it.

These days life is still hard. And a few years later, it's still a chore to reason and function in the hurricane season. I awaken to a broken heart every day. And the winds still blow, but maybe not at hurricane levels every day. But they kick up pretty often and I guess that's just our weather forecast, our reality. We may as well get used to it.

HERE IS A VISIT FROM JUNE 21, 2018.

Hi Dad, I'm here. The flute is a different vibration here. That's how we hear music through a vibration. I like it. The hats came. It's now a routine. Less manic, more smooth this year. I will let you know if it will go forever. Time will tell and so will I. Just a cool outing. Keep it smooth Pop. I love the book. I pushed you yesterday to look into the agents and publishers. Find the route and talk to people. That's how you roll. It will get through & you need to be ready to hang on. Like the roller coaster at Great America. Sit in and put on the seat belt. I'm driving Pop. It will be a good time for both of us. Look back on these notes when we are standing on a beach together at night with the moon shining. Know I put it into motion. Not just for us but for other dads & their kids here. They want to shake their dads because they are right here. Right next to them. But they can't hear or see or smell them. But it's all there.

Great job Dad, way to go. I miss you Pop. I always felt at home around you. Feel that way all the time now. You'll see. The people you need will walk in your path. Don't worry about money, it will cross your path also. It will allow you to do what you are supposed to do. Carry the message and open the door to the other side. Dude, it's me. Did you think you wrote that well? Yeah, try again. I'm helping, I'm guiding. I'm not your spirit guide but I can guide you & will through the rest of your days. Getting in a flow, aren't you? It's me Pop! Don't be silly. The connection is forever. And the service work to break the barrier even helps more. Remember this moment when you are on a stage talking to brokenhearted parents. We can heal them together or at least ease their pain. I'm really proud of you. Give Bailey a hug from me Sunday. He's a big sweet bull of a kid. He loved me and I will visit him sometime when he is ready. I cleared the path so you can have a free & easy weekend with Al and your pals. I love them because they love you. It's a pass through, get it? I'm happy Dad, know that. It's so cool to travel back and forth to you and back to my world. It's called paradise for a reason. You'll see. The kids are doing better. I was guiding them where they would let me. It will happen. Tell Momma I love her so very much. She's my mom and will always be. Wow, can I feel her love. Didn't know how to accept it before. But I do know. It's all about love on both sides, nothing else. The rest is bull. Nothing else.

Spread it Pop. Make somebody's day today & think of me. I'll be right next to you. Let's meet with Andrew next week. Good strong visit.

Love you so much
C

Well, that doesn't require a lot of explanation. A flute played during this meditation. Chris explains vibrations. He also talks about the upcoming golf outing in September and a college friend visit approaching on Sunday at his grave. The amazing thing is everything he foretells in this visit comes true. The book getting published, countless interviews, and presentations with grieving parents in the audience. My boy sees it all. He sends his mom love of course. He talks about coming to me, which he did a few days before on June 13, 2018. He tells me he enjoys going back and forth between worlds. He is something.

JULY 7, 2018

Hi Dad,

I had to go. It wasn't working any more. They knew, He knew. It was time for me to go home. You will know when it's your time. Nothing sad or empty about it. Like coming home. Packing to travel, making plans. But walking off the plane, I'm always home when I see you. That's how it is Pop, home. I'm where we all started & where we all come back to. Just like home. I always knew how much you loved me and that's the same way here. But even more. You did a great job so let go of any sorrow or regret. I'm here because I love you. Would I come back to you if you didn't do a great job? With all I have here I still miss you and my mom. That means a lot. Some people just cross and that's it. Get it?

You're on a beach in your head, right? Me too. Listen to the water and look at the crescent- shaped moon. I'm looking at it. We share the same moon Dad. I'll be at Gina's with all my friends. Love them Dad, they are me. A part of me is in their hearts. Wow, I was loved. So grateful for that. You are too. Over here also. You made a great journey of your life. Done some good things Pop. Attunement will be a breeze. A few missed steps but you more than made up for them. Thanks for getting up Pop. You know now, right? Push the book. Walk the walk.

I love you
Chris.

What a wonderful visit and message. He lovingly lets me know he has to go. I love the fact that he says he went home, and that home is a wonderful place where he is loved. Like his home in our world but even more so. And we are all going. He wants me to let go of any regret. I have to believe that message is for all parents in our shoes. I love that he still misses me and his mom. We did go to his darling friend Gina's college graduation party and spent some wonderful time with her and all his friends. Yeah, just like he says. He was all around us (mostly them) at the party. What helps immensely with my grief is that he sounds so content. A grounded, loving, contemplative contentedness. In other words, he's good. He tells me when my time comes my attunement "will be a breeze." I knew attunement wasn't the same as atonement which in my mind denotes judgement. So, I looked it up. Google defines attunement like this:

"Attunement is intended to connect a person more closely to their spiritual source and to open the flow of life current."

That fits. That will work.

A few years later, while writing this book down in Florida, I of course find myself on a beach at night, looking up at the stars and moon in total awe. I ask Chris for a sign and the song that comes on in my Jeep is Brad Paisley's "Anything Like Me." It's a song about an expectant dad thinking "heaven help us" if his boy is anything like him. Chris turned me on to Brad Paisley and that song would make me cry before Chris crossed over, but since … well you get it. If you're a dad. Do yourself a favor and sit back, listen to the song, and let the tears flow. It will be good for you, even though it can hurt like hell.

ON JULY 10, 2018, I HAD A PHONE READING WITH SHERI JEWEL.

I'm looking in my notes and I think this was an impromptu phone reading with Sheri Jewel. See, really good mediums (good in their craft and good in their heart) will do that. So many people are critical of mediums for charging for a session and that's crazy. Do therapists work for free? Of course not. Now, I agree some big-time mediums gouge a bit, but that's between them and their conscience. It's not me to judge. However, personally speaking, even when I have paid a tidy sum for a reading it was worth every penny. But the mediums in my life really care. They care about me, and they care about Chris. They care about my family, and they care about my journey. How cool is that? I consider Andrew Anderson, Sheri Jewel, and Toni Russo dear friends. I am so very fond of Jill Nicole and have connected with Suzanne Giesemann. After pursuing her to read my book (just this side of stalking actually), I did a radio interview with her and she subsequently did a reading for me, where Chris came shining through. That was amazing and so very kind. That's who these people are. They are in the business of helping. They are in the business of healing. They are in the business of connecting souls. So, please people, save your skepticism and judgement around me. They, as it was so sappily stated in Jerry McGuire, complete me. So, here is the reading:

Kerry was a guide. She is a mother figure on the other side. His protector. Dad, I love you. It happened so quick. A split second. Sheri tells me there is nothing to worry about with Chris as he's got his shit together (note: Sheri doesn't mince words). You might meet him again, on this side. I will know it's him by the eyes. He drank too much, had mild depression, and some erratic behavior. Boys will be boys. He's an amazing energy. I should copyright the book (first book), and there is more to come. How to survive grief and loss after losing a child. He walks with you every day. Oneness. His spirit is always around me. Find the laughter and joy again. Who worked on the railroad? Sheri mentions his friend Pat who crossed with him. Using his last name which I won't do. "You're the best dad possible. He's like your rock." Sheri asked me, "Do you have his phone?" (yes) and "Do you have his flask?" (no).

These kids (his friends) think of you as a dad. They liked driving with you to hockey games. He knew you were there.

He loves his mother and is around her a lot. Around the family. An eternal part that bonds. Are you in his bedroom? He walks the Ranch. He mentions a fire pit. I see a plaque. Is there a fire pit?

She mentions a graduation tassel, a brown bracelet, and asks if I have a tattoo. He says, "I'm a joker, I'm a smoker, I'm a midnight toker." He tells me I'm the best daddy in the world.

He mentions the Prologue of my book and he mentions his mom. He's around her, too. Equally. Sheri says he acknowledges the family stands behind him.

What an amazing drive-by reading. It was just peppered with accuracy and full of Chris's spirit. Sheri mentions Kerry—we will go into that relationship a little later. But this made total sense. Sheri asked who worked on the railroad. And that's a reference to Chris's Grandfather Iron Joe who is with him on the other side. He lets me know he considered me a great dad. And that fills my heart with joy. He mentions his friend Pat, who crossed with him, the cell phone we keep, and my relationship with his friends. He brings up the fire pit and a plaque. In 2018, we went to In Balance Ranch for a fundraiser and the Barrassos surprised us by dedicating a newly built fire pit to Chris. Along with a plaque. I mean, come on people, are you with me on all this? I always felt he was his very best on the Ranch. And I know a part of him will always be there.

She then mentions a graduation tassel and a brown bracelet. Chris's graduation cap, complete with tassel, hangs on my bookcase. The brown leather bracelet that says, "Dad," first mentioned in my first meeting with Andrew, is clamped to my Jeep's steering wheel. We don't have a flask of his, but on one of the first Chris McQ Pub Crawls—celebrated around his April 15 birthday which he shares with his dear friend Bailey—we did give Bailey a monogrammed flask. Maybe, but I don't know for sure. But it seems to fit.

He ends with a reference to Steve Miller's song the "Joker." It makes me smile because years later, his spirit is the same sweet, loving, funny, young man.

Man, I miss him!

A Tribute to

Christopher Joseph Mcquillen

"For those who love with their heart and soul there is no such thing as separation."

Chris has passed, but the joy he has brought to the lives he has touched lives on. His legacy is the gift of joy and for that we are forever grateful. You will always be part of our family.

-Love the Barrasso's

CHAPTER TWELVE:

I Didn't Know It Was Ok

I was taking a cigar break at work with my pal Jeff, a dear, dear friend. Jeff and I work together, and we have known each other for over thirty-five years. We both came from the car business and had clawed our way up to be car dealers. So, we had the same tenacious work ethic. And because of that, we shared very similar successes in our current life. It was the end of the year, and it had been particularly rewarding. Actually, it had been financially the best year of my career, any career. The year had worked on a number of fronts: Caroline was doing so well; Will was back in college at Boulder with a new-found attitude about learning; and Sally's practice was booming. Even the smaller things were working out. I had found the perfect gift for William for Christmas. It was a sterling silver and 10k gold family crest ring. It was of course the McQuillen crest, which had been tattooed on both Chris's and William's biceps. And it was being made and shipped and would arrive well before Christmas. See, things were working out.

On another front, COVID-19 had taught a lot of us who never knew it that we could work remotely. And being particularly old school, I was late to the party. By choice. I thought I had to have my hands on every aspect of a deal. Start to finish. Well that all changed. And because business had been so robust, I agreed to take on an assistant.

Also, Caroline—after graduating from college, and a semester of student teaching—was finally teaching grammar school in Milwaukee. But that industry was a mess with COVID. She had been wrestling with the idea of moving back to Chicago and possibly taking a break from teaching and trying real estate sales. I had a number of wonderful female agent friends who I thought would be great mentors if she decided to pursue this. However, the idea began to creep in that she could come in with me. I had this amazing book of business that I (yeah, all me) had built up over the last dozen years, and I wasn't getting any younger. Because I had gotten into residential mortgages after the 2008 crash, a lot of brokers had left the industry leaving an opening for someone like me. It really worked out. If she chose to join me, it could be a wonderful solution to both of our current situations. She wanted to make more money, and I couldn't stop the sands of time from shifting. So, after speaking with Sally about it, the next day I called Caroline and brought it up. She had already thought about it and had looked into the requirement to secure licensing. What? How in literally God's name did that happen? So, check.

On top of this I had just had a successful hip replacement in November. The week before, I flew to Florida with Rick, and we joined Allen for ninety holes of golf in four days. I wanted to get all the mileage I could out of the old hip before getting it replaced. I did; check. Because of the surgery, I was working exclusively from home for a week and a half. Remember, Sally works out of the house. Thus, I was underfoot. So, I was temporarily disabled, cooped up at home with winter setting in. Sally likes working from home. She likes her routine and surprisingly my presence can be disruptive, to say the least. We needed a plan. And here it was: maybe I could drive to Florida and stay a few weeks. Maybe I could drive to Florida and stay a month.

I could work remotely, have the kids join me separately as to have one-on-one time with each of them. Maybe Sally would consider joining me for a week. It seemed crazy, no it didn't, it made perfect sense. I could work, have time with the kids, and even finish this book. Our second book. I could finish it while visiting the beaches I so loved. The beaches that have become a thin place for us.

But it's a lot of moving parts and a big ask for Sally. I approached Sally about my newest Wiley Coyote type plan. I don't think I got the entire plan out when she blurted, "That's a great idea, you should do that." I was overwhelmed with gratitude. My wife was recognizing how hard I had worked and was deserving of this outlet. Or maybe it was that I was such a pain in the ass around the house that a 1,352-and-a-half-mile journey was just the solution!

OK so now, I was on it. I really wanted to spend at least part of the trip at my sister's house in Naples, Florida. It was a wonderful place where we went annually as a family and where I ran to for comfort when things got tough—before and after Christopher transitioned (another catchy term). We had gone there when the kids were small. Chris loved it there as a kid (who wouldn't?) with his Aunt Marcia making him feel special and absolutely spoiling him. He continued to show up when he was a young man whenever his little jaunts took him to the sunshine state. I knew I could write there. I knew Chris's spirit and now Marcia's moved freely there. It is only now that I am realizing I will be at her home on the second anniversary of her crossing on February 6. But I am getting ahead of myself. I do that. So, I reached out to my precious niece Colleen to inquire about the availability. Although she had tentatively committed to renting it to some friends-of-friends of Marcia's from February through April, maybe she could push them back till the second half of the month. Bam, done. The friend had agreed. I had a place to stay that was precious to me, I had a new hip that would be ready for golf by February 1, and I had a hall pass for this road trip that was beginning to feel like Jack Kerouac meets Travels with Charlie.

I planned on staying at Marcia's for three weeks, and then one week on Siesta Key. (I ended up staying almost two full months in Florida. But who's counting?) I rented a place on the beach so Sally could spend a week with her feet in the sand (quartz crystal actually). This was actually happening. All of this had come together as well as me stumbling on the perfect gifts for everyone I love. Including a medium reading by phone for my niece Colleen with Andrew Anderson, while her family was celebrating Christmas in Naples at Marcia's home (actually, it was their second home now).

All of this was falling into place. Business, family, Christmas, and a road trip. Check, check, check, check.

While relating this to Jeff, a mood must have come over me because he said, "It's ok to be happy you know." I didn't know. I didn't know it was ok to be happy. I had spent the previous years after Chris's death dreading the holidays. I was miserable from Thanksgiving—hell, maybe even Halloween—until my birthday on January 9. We buried my boy on January 8, 2016. We do however have an amazing celebration at his grave and then at our house on the anniversary of his crossing on January 3, and it took place this year despite COVID. We pulled off the golf outing, didn't we? And although the celebration of Chris's life feeds my soul, it also breaks my heart in two. But I was and am feeling happy. I don't miss or grieve him less. I still visit the grave, cry, and write. But I found room in my heart and life for happiness again. And I know it's not a betrayal. I know it's my path. My path someday back to my boy.

I HAD THIS VISIT FROM CHRIS ON JULY 18, 2018:

Hi Pop. It still works Dad. I'm with you. I sent you Naples, so you know it's me. You are a great Dad. So, let it all go. See my friends this weekend. Their love makes me smile. I'm in my prime Pop. Always will be. Sometimes I walk with Casey on the beach. She loves you too. Your love was like a laser beam. I didn't know how special that was. Especially as a kid. It was so strong and still is. I'll line things up for the book. Do it on your own. I'll help just like the golf outing. You got this, and I got this. So cool. Like Will's lacrosse net. Stay pure Pop. White light working on you. Thanks Dad. I feel the love this very moment. It comes through. I'm glad we did this. You needed this. The book ended, the outings end, but....

Good meditation. It's the beach in Sarasota. Strong energy. Strong mojo. I know you miss me, but I'm right next to you. I'll golf with you today. Remember to look. Remember to feel it. I'm really happy Dad, but I'm sorry you hurt so much. Your love comes through like a white beam to me. I'm proud my Dad loves me so much.

If you get a chance in Canada, give the towel to Karen and tell her Jerry is over here and loves her. He's so proud of her. He's such a great guy. He's still my uncle here. I know it hurts but the connection is so strong that you know it won't go away. I know that and you sometimes know that. Like right now. Right? Our time Pop. 3:00–4:00 a.m. I'm not sad anymore. It's better for me, but I know it's hard to keep going for you. Soon enough Dad. As hard as you worked to put the book together, now let's get it published and start phase 2. I'm behind you and guiding you. Stay in the light like the moon beam on the gulf that night. You can see it right now. Stay in the beam and I'll guide you here. It's about me.

Wrap it up Dad.
I love you now & love you forever.
Chris

Well once again, he just nails it. I've been told by Andrew that he always will be in his prime. I love that. He was so friggin' gorgeous. His mass card photo is on my dashboard, and I just get lost in his beauty. I might be biased but I don't think so. I love how he is with our old dog Casey. I never questioned either of their love for me. I was obviously worried about the first book getting published and he says he'll handle it. He does. He mentions the meditation and the beach in Sarasota. Good mojo. I guess it's no coincidence I'm writing this chapter on a balcony overlooking Siesta Key Beach. The coincidence or lack thereof makes me smile.

Chris mentions a towel for his cousin Karen. He's referring to a black golf towel with the McQ crest emblazoned on it. I ordered a handful a while back and ended up with an extra. One, of course, hung on Chris's golf bag. At the last golf outing, I noticed my nephew Mike and all his boys had white ones with the crest (mine were cooler). So, Chris decided the golf towel should go to his cousin Karen. Mike's sister. And that was that. Mike, Karen, and Kathy were my adored brother Jerry's kids. A little side note. Karen is joining her brother and nephews at the Chris McQ Annual Golf Outing. See, circling the wagons.

Jerry transitioned in June of 2014. Chris went with me to attend the funeral and help with his Aunt Marcia who was for the most part wheelchair bound. Looking back, I am so grateful for that time. I was with two of my favorite people in the world, together to honor another favorite. Chris says that Jerry is with him. Or he is with Jerry. He mentions that Jerry still holds the rank of his uncle, even on the other side. Selfishly, I love this as it means that I will hold the rank of "Dad" when I cross. There is nothing on this side or the other that makes me happier than being Chris's dad.

Another wonderful aspect of Jerry's funeral was that I reconnected with my cousin Teresa. Jerry loved Teresa and wanted us to be friends. It took a couple of years and a local hockey tournament for us to really connect. But we did. Not only does Teresa and her family (especially my nephew Paul) add tremendously to my life, but I believe it makes Jerry happy. And it was really his doing. Jerry always looked out for all of us. And he wants us to look out for each other. Yeah, Jerry is a strong spirit.

But back to the towel. When we got to Canada a few weeks after this visit, I gave Karen her towel and delivered her dad's message. I believe I saw a tear in her eye. Of course, I did. She's an Irish lass.

Another little side note. The following year, Karen and her entourage of friends journeyed to the Windy City for a long weekend. They honored me by asking me to join them for lunch at a place on the river walk. I had immediately arranged to have the bill for the group given directly to me. When the meal was over and Karen realized what had happened, she said, "You didn't have to do that Uncle Joey." "Karen," I asked, "what would your dad think if I didn't grab the check?" "You're right Uncle Joey," was her response, "and thank you." I love that kid. See Jerry, just following your lead.

CHAPTER THIRTEEN:

I WAS COFFEE AND SHE WAS TEA

That was the response to my question of why a relationship ended, posed to an old sponsor of mine thirty-five years ago. The guy's name was Eli, and he was a very spiritual cat. He was a kind of knock-around guy who was successfully recovering from both drug and gambling addictions. He was winning both battles all the way to the other side. Eli was dating a gal who was a bit out of his social class. A nice gal who, like Eli was working hard on her own recovery and self-improvement. But although we were all hopeful, none of us could see Eli at the spring cotillion at her daddy's country club. Not that she necessarily belonged to one, but you get where I'm going here. So, it fizzled out. But I always remember that seven-word description of their doomed relationship. Kind of poetic, but right to the point. Eli, one time held court and discussed the artistic beauty of Joni Mitchell album titles. Think about it. "Wild Things Run Fast" or "Chalk Mark in a Rainstorm." You got to give it to him. He had real insight and the soul of a poet.

About fifteen years later, I had moved to the suburbs and lost track of Eli. I heard through the grapevine he had cancer, and that it was terminal. I rooted around and either found or was provided with his cell phone number. Probably the latter, because when I was hanging with Eli cell phones didn't exist yet.

So, I called Eli and when he answered his voice took me back to a simpler time. A sweet time. I told him I heard the news and how sorry I was. I asked him how much time he had left. "Oh man!" he said, "That's so you. Everyone else tap dances around the subject and you just come out and ask. I love you, Joe."

That's it, that's the point. Eli's cancer wasn't going to go away if I didn't acknowledge it. And it's the same with parents who've lost kids. We want to be asked about it. "How are we handling it? How are the other kids doing?" We want you to speak their name, and maybe even tell us a story about an interaction with them. Putting your head down or turning away is not an expression of love.

Recently, Sally had an interaction with a friend who had lost her husband a few years back. Coming from a place of understanding and love, Sally acknowledged how tough the holidays must be for her and asked how she was doing. "Thank you," her friend said. "Thanks for acknowledging and caring. Thanks for mentioning his name."

That woman sent Sally an email with a photo of two beer cans from the first Chris McQ Golf Outing. The labels on the can were specific to the outing with a photo of Chris on them. My friend Mike had two pallets of them delivered to the first golf outing. Anyway, Sally's friend had a refrigerator in her garage full of beer. Something happened and all the bottles and cans of beer exploded. Every single one. Well almost. The only survivors were the two cans of Chris McQ beer left over from the outing. A few days later in an impromptu reading with Sheri Jewel, she asked me why she was seeing two cans of beer surrounded by exploded ones in a refrigerator. I don't know if the message was from Chris or Dan, but it was from the other side and it was loud and clear.

We can share the burden, and others can help with our load. It doesn't change our reality. Our Thanksgiving with an empty chair or a Christmas morning with one less participant... but it makes a difference. It helps.

"We talk about them not because we're stuck or we haven't moved on, but we talk about them because we are theirs, and they are ours, and no passage of time will ever change that."
~Scribbles & Crumbs

CHAPTER FOURTEEN:

A PERFECT MOMENT

The Latin word, **Inspiritus**, means "to breathe." As in to breathe spirit into.

To be filled with the spirit. It is the root for the word inspiration and in the creative sense, it means to be filled with the spirit. To be filled with the Source.

If we want to connect... we need to be filled with the spirit.

I have been asked about the meditation part of connecting with my son Chris. During a session with him yesterday at 3:30 a.m., he sent me a memory. He called it a perfect moment. It was November 2010 and I picked him up in Tucson and we drove to Scottsdale. We stayed in Old Scottsdale, and we explored the town, ate like kings, and binge-watched hotel movies at night. We were happy. He was content. During meditation, I focused on that moment. And he came through... clearly. Later in the morning, I dug through pictures and found one I knew was there of him at that moment, laying safe and content. So, the reason for this chapter is that Chris wants you to do the same: *Focus on a perfect moment.* The love you feel at that moment you remember, will help promote communication. I promise.

ON JULY 27, 2018 CHRIS CAME THROUGH.

Twin Flames Pop. That's you & Me. I know more and am paving the way. But you're still my dad. Always will be. Your dad energy. My son energy. Forever Pop, that's the way it is. So my guides on both sides. Follow them. You know the difference. That's intuition. A knowing that's part of you. Good meditation Dad, really good. Full moon tonight. You knew we would be talking. I knew it too. I missed you Pop. We've been talking and that's the advantage you have. It's been ongoing and will always continue. The book is on path. You follow the path I'm laying out. Thanks for having the faith in me. When you see a medium or healer you know when it's my or their energy. That's a gift. Like intuity. Follow up. The door to write is now open. Allow it to open fully. I'll always be next to you when you write. (Behind you, more accurately.) Look for me in Canada. I'll be there. I'll be in the family. Look for me in the moon & the waves. I love you Pop. Look for me on the beach. I'll be with you, don't worry. I love you as much as you love me. But I know I'll see you again. You hope it. Get to the knowing. It will come.

Pulling Back,
Love you
Chris

Well, that doesn't require much explaining, does it? One thing that kind of confirms that these messages aren't from me is that Chris uses the word 'intuity.' I wasn't sure intuity was a word, and neither was spell check, by the way. But I looked it up. And it sure does fit.

Intuity refers to a person's ability to intuit, similar to 'intuitiveness' but not identical. Intuity refers to general ability, intuitiveness refers to capability. In the word ‹acute› there is ‹acuity.'

ON AUGUST 10, 2018 CHRIS CAME THROUGH.

Hi Dad,

I'm still here. Don't doubt. I'm around you. Casey is here with me wagging her tail and smiling at you. We shared a feeling that you would always take care of us Dad. We both always trusted you Dad. Missing you too. Get to a beach at night this weekend & I'll meet you. Bring Cassidy. She'll see and feel me. Look for your spirit guide Pop. It's about time you find him/her. Time to seek them out. You'll recognize that they've always been there. Next level Pop. Hypnotics etc. You know what to do. You got this now push yourself. The book is in play. You did most of the work so you need to expand on this. Spiritual enlightenment, soul enlightenment. It's exciting and you need exciting now. Get off your ass Pop & help people, by expanding who you are. You just needed a little wake-up call. Now you got it.

See you on the beach,
Love
Chris

Ok, so I guess I was just taken out to the proverbial spiritual woodshed. It's time to kick my spiritual growth into second gear. I didn't think I was a slacker, but my boy thinks my growth is important to be able to help others. So, I'm in.

AUGUST 25, 2018

Hi Dad,

Been a while. I'm always here. Getting things ready for Marcia. No sadness. She will be with us. We love her and we're getting ready for her to come home. It will be home for you. But not yet Dad. Not yet. I love Al. He's a good friend. There is a soul connection. You'll figure it out later. That's why you are so comfortable. You and I have that. But even stronger. Soul family, twin flames. It's a forever thing. Not just a lifetime. I walked through the airport with you. I held you as you rode down the elevator. I miss you too Pop. But, really, really, happy.

Moving to different levels, but that doesn't put a distance between us. That won't change. But I am quickly advancing, like the water and fire levels. But I was always connected to you. See, it makes sense. Your spirit animal is a wolf. But a domesticated one. One that is in the process of domestication. It's not wild. Even though we were. We were just being chased by something. I'm at peace, totally at peace. I'm content, completely content. I had it briefly at the Ranch. Now it's all the time. Be happy for me, Dad. I'm hugging you right now. Feel it? I'm not your spirit guide but we are connected too. So, you can use me like one. It works.

Don't sweat the outing, it will be a great time. I'll be around my friends instead of golfing with you. But you get it. Look close when they are together & you'll see me. I promise. Yeah, that's

*right. Good to commit. Look forward to Thomas John today. I'll
be there. Life and ink, right?*

*Love
Chris*

This is a very cool visit. He talks about the family preparing for
his Aunt Marcia's return home—her transition that took place
not all that long after on February 6, 2019. I was in Naples,
Florida visiting her, and my dear friend Allen drove down to hang
with me and say goodbye to her. Chris lets me know that I'll be
welcomed home by family when I cross. He talks about moving
to a new level. He makes reference to water and fire. When he
was at In Balance Ranch, the kids moved up to different levels
of sobriety and spirituality, which were indicated by elements.
Fire and water and a few more that escape my memory. But the
process of his spiritual advancement makes sense when he puts
it that way. He lets me know what my spirit animal is and talks
about spirit guides during our last visit. So, we need to look into
them both. The strongest message he has for me was that he is
happy. At peace and content. Content is not a normal state for a
McQuillen. But he is there, and I'm getting there. Also, Thomas
John had to reschedule for another day. It was a bit disappointing.
But well worth it. Chris ends it with, "life and ink, right?"

That's a line from a Jimmy Buffett song about the author
William Faulkner. The line is "Life and ink they run out at the
same time, or so said my old friend the squid." I love that line.
And I know what he's telling me. I'll be writing with him at my
side till it's my time. Sounds good to me, buddy.

Let's take a look at both spirit guides and spirit animals.

SPIRIT GUIDES

First, let's explore spirit guides. Wikipedia defines them as follows:

> *A spirit guide, in western spiritualism, is an entity that remains as a disincarnate spirit* to act as a guide or protector to a living *incarnated* human being.

And here's how Gaia defines spirit guides:

> *Guides are any spiritual beings that help you at any time during your life for any length of time to become a better person.* Guides may present themselves when you are in a stressful situation or have been with you your entire life.

> I have been using Chris as my guide. And I think it's ok. He has inferred that my guide helps him guide me, and maybe he even sends me their messages because he knows I will listen to him. But now he wants me to find my guide. So, I will. Meanwhile, let's explore spirit animals.

SPIRIT ANIMALS

According to Google, here is how spirit animals are defined:

> A **spirit animal** is characterized as a teacher or messenger that comes in the form of an animal and has a personal relationship to an individual. Other names might be animal guides, spirit helpers, spirit allies, power animals, or animal helper.

And here's how Gaia defines them:

Spirit Animals share information you need to help you balance and grow in your life. The qualities of a Spirit Animal are all the inherent attributes of the particular animal's entire species. As you research a particular species, you understand which qualities of talents the Spirit Animal is suggesting that you adopt for your benefit in order to grow in your life.

In the visit, Chris tells me my spirit animal is a wolf. But a mostly domesticated one. Or one at least on the way to domestication. I think that's interesting, as I am drawn to wolves. However, not long ago, I was in a gallery on 5th Avenue in Naples and saw a carving of a Polar Bear that really called to me. On Caroline's urging, I bought it. Rubbing it with my hands or simply looking at it gives me peace and calms me down.

So, perhaps as with spirit guides, you may have one or more spirit animals, too. I guarantee you more will be revealed to me. And I will pass it on. Stay tuned!

SEPTEMBER 14, 2018

Hi Dad,

Great event. Kind of wild that that it's in my honor. Thanks for that. It was a full day. Even when you were engaged in the event, I was with you. All around. I like the baby picture but that's not me. I'm just like I was when I left you on January 2. I'm always 21 here. That's how you will always see and remember me. I'm not leaving you Pop. I'm just around you. You have to tap into energy. Hard to explain. You can't hear the music without headphones, and you can't hear me without tapping in.

Lay down the worries Pop. We know it's not a long run on your side. I'll bring you home soon enough. Thanks for bringing

Gali. That was a special love. I will watch out for her. Such a pure love for her. From her. Thanks for coming to the grave yesterday. I know you were tired, and I loved the lantern. It rose up. I told my friends on my side that it was from my dad. You are trying so hard Pop. Lisa is a literary guide not just an agent. I connect with her. I can tap into her and she to me. It's your book, my book. It's our book Pop. It will touch the brokenhearted. It will heal those broken souls. Dad, let go of any thoughts you let me down. I've only got love for you. You did the best anyone could. I can still feel the love across the divide. I just sent a chill, so you know I'm here. I was restless there. I'm not now. I can sit and be with you. No time here. You'll see. Listen to the meditation. I'm looking through the glass wall in the American terminal. It's me coming home to you. But you gotta know I'm home here, and you will be too. Kiss the baby picture and put it away. I'm with Will. He's ok now. I'll take care of Caroline. Needs dam to burst. So much pain. Not just because of me. Energy Pop. All energy. White light & love. It fills the space. It's love. You were the finest man I knew Pop. You always loved me and I always felt safe. I knew I could come to you, that no matter what you loved me. That's something I carry with me. That's love wrapped around me. Tough for you to understand. But you will Pop. Just not right now. Write Caroline a letter and tell her she's loved. I'll send her love through energy. She will feel it. I promise. This is a good meditation. The cardinal, the path, the forest. I love you Pop. I'll be with you all day today. I'll soothe you and let you know it's all good.

Keep walking this path to me.
Love You
Chris

Well, Chris enjoyed his golf outing surrounded by his loving, loyal friends. And so did I. But of course, it always hurts a little, or a lot. He tells me to kiss the picture of him as a baby. So, let me explain. When I meditate prior to his visits, I always pull out a photo. And this time I pulled out a photo of him as little boy. I began to think all parents miss their little ones when they grow up, but for us parents whose kids have crossed over it's worse. A lot worse. Chris reminds me that he is viewed as the twenty-one-year-old boy (beautiful boy). And when I join him that's how he will look to me. He says he will look the same as when he left on January 2. I double-checked my notes, and that was it—January 2. So, he means the last time I saw him in the flesh, before he headed to Wisconsin. He makes reference to me being the finest man he knew. And I am complimented and oh so proud. But that statement also confirms these comments aren't originating from me. I would never refer to myself that way. Don't get me wrong. I'm a good guy. I am a big fan of me, but I certainly wouldn't put myself in the finest man category. Although I'm glad he does.

He makes reference to the American glass wall. I had mentioned before that I would wait for him outside the glass security wall of America and we both would beam when we saw each other through the glass. When I meditate at his grave I look into the woods and imagine that glass wall, and that smile. But I've told you that before. A few times. Maybe more than a few. It's part of the process. And it's important. He talks about the Chinese lantern I released at his grave. This is a good lesson. Anything we do to honor our kids is recognized by them. Keep it up. Do more. I know I intend to.

CHAPTER FIFTEEN:
_____

THE FIRSTS ARE THE WORST

In the last session, Chris talked about his brother and sister. And this is a good time (though there's never really a good time) to talk about siblings of the ones who cross early. Let me begin by saying that Chris was a great son. A great friend and a staunch ally. But he wasn't a great older brother to Caroline or Will. He was impatient and his indifference or criticism cut them both to the quick. I really believe that while he was struggling, he felt everything came easy to his younger siblings. But it's like a duck gliding effortlessly across a pond. It's not really effortlessly at all. But all the paddling is below the surface. That's the way it was for Caroline and Will. They accomplished things through hard work. But Chris couldn't appreciate it then. Both of their issues with losing an older brother and their grief, is their story, and I respect their privacy. But I know that Chris was getting closer to them both. And that made his exit even more painful. Caroline said in a candid moment about Chris. "We were finally getting close… and then he died." It truly broke my heart. I know Will felt the same way. Will wrote a paper about it for his freshman year at Boulder, and it was an incredibly well-written piece. When we were together in Florida recently, I asked his permission to put it in the book. And he agreed. So, here goes, exactly as he wrote it.

THE FIRSTS ARE THE WORST

By Will McQuillen

I snapped to my feet. I had been awoken by the noise that continued to haunt me for the next three years. A piercing shriek followed by a sorrowful stream of tears. This noise came from the person I love most. The most supportive, warm, and kind person I know. My Mother. I never figured that something my Mom could do would end up in my nightmares. That night it echoed through my freshly awoken mind, feeling like I had the dreaded "wake up" alarm embedded into my head. This time I was dreaming, but the day prior I wasn't, I heard it for real.

Just as I did every time I was about to drive, I fiddled with the aux cord until my music wasn't secondary to static. I was used to this annoying routine, but usually I'd be attempting to blast Kodak Black, 21 Savage, and J Cole, not Jimmy Buffett, James Taylor and John Denver. I've always had a deep appreciation for both types of music but when it comes to being in the car, it's usually rap. That day was different, it felt right to shuffle the playlist I dedicated to him the year before. I finally pulled into the cemetery, we only live about ten minutes from it, but that time the drive felt like an hour.

As I stepped out of my brother's 2010 black Jeep Wrangler, I zoned in on the group of 50 + people who had gathered on January 3rd, 2017, on a sub-freezing day in the suburbs of Chicago. We were all there to celebrate and honor the first anniversary of my brother Chris's death. I made my way to the trunk and took a look at the Buffalo Bills Logo on the tire cover (the cover that has since been removed because local police recognize the car from it…oops), mustered up my one and only smile of the day, for me, not for anyone else, and lifted the cooler out from the trunk. It was a painful day, I loved that everyone was there for my brother and the rest of the family, but seeing all of his frat brothers who share his personality type was so hard that it stung. Each conversation I had with them just made me think more and more that I shouldn't even know these people. Chris should've been with all them hanging out at the AKL frat house, living life like a college kid and I should've been just an irrelevant Fraternity brother's sibling. Chris had so many amazing qualities, he was the life of the party and always showed love to the underdog. He was my older brother, I always looked up to him, I wanted to be just like him in so many ways while also learning from the multitude of mistakes he made in his life. As I stood there surrounded by the ones who loved him most, I was repeatedly told "you two have the same laugh," "the older you get, the more you look like him," and lastly "he'd be so proud of you." Hearing that put me down more than it picked me up. I knew he wouldn't have been proud of me, there was nothing to be proud of. I was doing really well before he drowned. I was star running back for football, a Division 1 recruited lacrosse player and my grades were great. I dropped off in every which way. I quit football, didn't care about grades, and put only half my heart into lacrosse. I felt like I had wasted that whole year absorbed in a sea of self-pity, and wasn't mentally able to get myself out of it. I've always been the "It's all good" guy, I didn't stress, I could shake off sadness and just always be relaxed. When we lost Chris, it activated my depression and affected my everyday life so drastically. Depression runs all the way through my family tree, but until Chris died, I never felt depressed, it was new for me and very overwhelming. That day I did what I do best, spew bullshit and tell people what they want to hear so they feel better.

I had the same conversation over and over, by the end of the day it truly felt scripted. I never initiated conversation, but when I had to speak it was only about how fine I was and how time heals everything, which at that time I didn't believe.

It was always tough for Chris and I to connect, especially as a kid. He was four-and-a- half years older than me and just always thought of me as the annoying little brother. I was annoying, even as a young kid I idolized him so I always tried to hang out with him and that usually just ended with a lot of disappointment. Growing up I was used to not having Chris around, but I still worshipped the ground he walked on. For his freshman year of high school in 2009, he was sent away to military school and that lasted about a semester. He was home living like a normal kid, until late as a sophomore he personally realized that he had alcohol and drug problems and was then sent away to Utah for 60 days of wilderness recovery. From wilderness he went straight to In Balance Ranch Academy in Tucson, Arizona, a rehabilitation school that is intended for kids with addictions. No phones, no outside contact, no alcohol, no drugs, only therapy and sobriety.

Upon his graduation, he got a job at the school and worked there until he moved out to Vermont following one of his best friends from the Ranch to manage his new band. Throughout that three-year process, there were only a couple of visits and a few monitored phone calls. I didn't know my brother anymore, I respected everything he had accomplished and his sobriety, but I sure didn't know him. I was proud of him, but I no longer admired him, I was mad at him for leaving me, I wanted to be the exact opposite of a person he was, and that's why I refused to experiment with alcohol and drugs until I was 17. I wanted to be nothing like him. That all quickly changed when I had my first personal exposure to death in 2013. My Aunt Kerry passed away shockingly from a brain aneurysm leaving her husband and two newly adopted 3- and 6-year-old sons from Korea behind. We all commuted to Buffalo, New York, for the funeral and Chris declared he was going to drop everything and move into their house to look after the two boys for a few months.

"Why'd you decide to do that?" I asked.

"It's family. Simple," Chris responded.

A flip switched, that was my brother. That was the guy I'm supposed to look up to.

All my life I just wanted a good big brother, someone to have my back, I wanted to be able to hang out with him and feel like it wasn't just a favor to my parents. It finally started, we were getting closer, it was so apparent how much I respected him and just wanted to be happy even though there was so much disappointment when he decided after three years that sobriety wasn't for him. He wanted to be a college kid, he wanted to drink with friends, he wanted to be normal. I was only 16, but I understood. Me and my freshly acquired license jumped at the invitation to go visit him at Northern Illinois University and go watch a football game.

I took my first step into his Fraternity house, quickly noticed that just about every room was trashed and littered with Busch Lites. "Damn man, this is a real piece of shit. Looks like your type of place."

"Fuck off, come upstairs to my humble abode," he replied.

Walking up the stairs excitedly, trying to avoid my feet getting stuck to the spilled beer on the stairs, headed to where my brother lived. The first person I met was Bailey.

He was sitting in Chris's room watching football on Chris's TV, and was taking a handle of SVEDKA to town. He shot me a smile and got up excitedly to shake my hand, and offered me the handle, I respectfully declined. "He's not a degenerate like us quite yet," Chris told Bailey (I guess he called I would be).

All of Chris's friends were super excited to get his 16-year-old little brother drunk, so that was a crusher for them. His friends kept filing in and out of the room to meet me and hang with us. To no surprise, I realized that my brother was the shit in their house, everyone loved him. I realized how happy he was, and it was unbelievable to share time with him in a place where he truly belonged. We hung out in his room sharing laughs until it was time to go to the game. The one thing we always had together was football, we both loved it and followed our Buffalo Bills, the rest of the NFL and college football in depth. With below freezing temperatures in Dekalb, we figured that the stadium would practically be empty, but we didn't care. We ignored the frigid wind and made the game fun for us by throwing out hilarious chirps to players on Central Michigan. That was the first time where I really felt like Chris enjoyed hanging out with me, and the trend continued for the next couple of months. We texted, called each other, hung out during thanksgiving and had a great time together at the start of winter break, I never felt closer to him. Soon after, during that same winter break, the scream that still haunts my dreams three years later, happened for real.

January 3rd, 2016. It was a normal Sunday for me, I woke up around 11:00 a.m. so I could watch the CBS pregame for the Bills. Not more than 20 minutes into it, my dad called me upstairs. I walked up expecting a full rundown of what the Bills needed to do to beat the Jets that week, but instead I was told, "Buddy, your brother is missing. You know he and a bunch of his friends were at Scotty's lake house partying. Chris and three friends were last reported going outside to smoke and a canoe was found flipped in the lake this morning. I'm headed up there right now." Honestly, I wasn't too worried, this was the same guy that fell down a 40-foot mine shaft in Arizona hiking, he fell on a ledge, if it was three feet to the right, his body would still be down there. He survived that. This was the guy that flipped his truck and came out of it only with a concussion. I truly believe in the concept of a guardian Angel, and Chris's was working overtime. I thought just one more time he'd be saved.

I continued on with my Sunday trying to distract myself, I watched the Bills game, stayed updated on my fantasy football team and just understood that nothing was in my control. My Mom on the other hand was beyond worried, that's her first-born son, with his life in question. I went upstairs again to check in on her and just be by her side along with my uncle Charlie, her brother. I laid with her like I used to when I was little, letting her hold me and play with my hair, just awaiting news. An hour went by and finally her cell phone rang. That's when I heard the scream, except I didn't just hear it, I felt it all throughout my body, it rung all over. Chris was dead and I didn't need to hear it from my dad on the phone to know. Chris and three of his high school buddies had all drowned.

My uncle had my mom handled, I was confused, I was pissed. I headed over to the umbrella stand by my back door that has only been used for my hockey sticks, lacrosse sticks, and baseball bats. I grabbed my lacrosse stick, I opened the sliding door and was greeted by the cold. I went down to my lacrosse net and just started hammering it with my stick. By the time I knew what I was doing, the steel shaft was in an "L" shape. That's just about all I remember from the day Chris died.

The firsts are the worst. They're the hardest to get through. His first Birthday without him, our first Christmas, first vacation, first anniversary, those were definitely the hardest checkpoints to pass. From when Chris first left for real, through my first experience with death, to the day he died, no matter how bad any of it may have been, I wouldn't be the person that I am today without taking those horrible moments and growing from them. "You gotta get through the bad to hit the good," my dad always tells me. I had to grow up fast because of all this, I find myself to be very mature. Chris taught me how to be a man and continues to this very day. One similarity that I know we had is that we were both old souls, and maybe that's why we bonded over the '70s music that fills my Spotify playlist dedicated to him, but maybe it's because I still want to take his good qualities and make them mine, I want to be just like him all over again. When I'm lost, I take a look at my left shoulder, it's graced with our family crest as a tattoo. Chris came up with the idea and got it when he was 17 in Tucson, so as a 17-year-old in Chicago, unbeknown to my parents I used his driver's license to pull off being over 18, and I got that I the same tattoo and added his initials. I know he comes through when I look at it and think about him, and how I know is because, "It's family. Simple."

CHAPTER SIXTEEN:

ALL US LONELY PEOPLE

*Timothy 6: For I am already being poured out like a libation,
and the time of my departure is at hand.*

*"I have fought the good fight, I have finished the race,
I have kept the faith."*

"THIS IS FOR ALL THE LONELY PEOPLE" ...

That's the opening line from a song by America. I was driving down the street last night and it came on the radio. *"This is for all the lonely people, thinking that life has passed them by. Don't give up until you drink from the silver cup. And ride that highway in the sky."* I remember seeing them in Erie, Pennsylvania in the fall of 1975, and they sang that song. Then it was just one of a bunch of good songs off their debut album. But forty-some years later, something struck a chord in me. I was lonely. I don't know if I have ever truly experienced loneliness before January 3, 2016. Sure, I have felt alone, or left out, or even hurt after being dumped (yeah that happened). But never lonely. That hole in your heart that by now you've come to accept will never go away. That's how it feels.

It's the start of the holiday season and I see college kids home for Thanksgiving, Christmas lights, lights being strung up, and the wet, nasty weather that indicates early winter in the Midwest.

With all those dominoes lined up it doesn't take much to set them all a tumbling. And there you are, in anguish over a verse from a song from a band whose other song included such memorable lines as, "in the desert you don't remember your name as there ain't no one for to give you no pain" … really!

I'm explaining this to you as though you've never felt your heart drop into your stomach, by a song, a photo, or just a memory. But my guess is that if you are reading this, you have. You've probably lost someone very special. And let's be clear: "lost" as in died. People in my world prefer transitioned or crossed over. But it's all the same. Someone who owned a piece of your heart, who ended their journey on this side. Someone who made you say, "When you left you took my heart with you." That's what happened. That's it in a nutshell. And here is what I've learned after nearly four years: it's OK.

I've learned so much. I've been exposed to so much. And I've received clear messages from the other side. And you know what? I've learned about grief, and those moments that take you out at the knees. I've learned it's ok. It won't kill you. It might feel like it will. And to be honest, sometimes you almost hope it will. But it doesn't; it subsides. Eventually, the tide rolls back out and you can restart your day. What I've also learned after this 1,400-plus day journey is that I'm not alone. I have my new pal Meghan who lost her infant son, my friend Tom who lost his high school-age son just over a year ago, my pal Matt who lost his two four-year-old boys, and Abigail's parents. And on and on.

"Ask me about the empty chair beside me
and I will gratefully tell you
all about the beautiful little boy
who should be sitting next to me,
the one who taught me how to stretch

my love

far and wide

enough to span the gap

between heaven and earth."

~Angela Miller, Contributor, *A Bed for My Heart*

(https://abedformyheart.com/product/mother-of-all-mothers/)

Of course, the loneliness and grief is not limited to those who've lost children. My arrogance has me believing that no grief is like the loss of a child. But that's my story. Yours may be about a spouse, a soulmate, a sibling.

Just sitting at a Thanksgiving dinner table still feels hollow and empty. It's those moments when you feel like you are on stage playing a part. That you are happy... but not. That you feel part of a larger family... but not. I have wonderful parts to play. I'm so lucky to be a father of my two kids on this side, and grateful for my loving, heartbroken wife. But what I really want at that moment is to be Christopher's dad, in the flesh. On this side of the veil. But I can't un-ring that bell, and I am now the person these events have caused me to be. And then as I'm making peace with my role, I feel him around me, or I get a sign.

The night I finished writing this chapter, or so I thought, I awoke in the early morning hours and a 1980s movie was on—a silly movie called *Footloose*. I was watching the movie and feeling sorry for myself and killing time before dawn when I saw a framed needlepoint hanging on the wall over the lead character's shoulder. I grabbed the remote and rewound the scene. And there, clear as day, was a bright-red needlepoint cardinal. It made me laugh, and it snapped me out of it, and I felt my son around me. I fell back asleep, remembering he isn't going anywhere.

CHAPTER SEVENTEEN:

DON'T STOP BELIEVING...

That title means so much to all of us who've lost loved ones. But once again, especially children. However, the words mean even more to Sally and me. When Chris was at NIU studying special ed, he worked with a theatre troupe of emotionally disabled young adults. They were called the Penguin Players and they, and their founders—the King family—remain very close to our hearts. Theirs is a cause we've picked up because of Chris. Just this morning, I jumped in my Jeep and the song "Don't Stop Believing" by Journey was blaring from the radio speakers. I began to cry so hard I could barely keep the Jeep going straight. Holy shite this came out of nowhere... or did it? "Don't Stop Believing" was the Penguin theme song and they ended their performances with all—cast crew, support staff, and audience—participating in a rousing rendition as Journey blared over the speakers in the halls. We were asked to present the Chris McQ Scholarship after Chris's death and in his memory to a deserving special ed student. I get chills remembering it. What I remember were the events after the show that Chris was part of. Because I didn't attend the inaugural show. I have beaten myself up pretty well over that.

I remember it like it was yesterday. I was laying on the couch watching football. Sally was going to the show and let me off the hook. It was the first Penguin Performance and Chris, as a mentor, had worked with one young performer over the previous months. The lad's name is Daniel. At the performance, the mentors dressed in black would back up the performers and perform a few numbers with their stewards. I have seen the video and it makes me proud, and also sad. The boring one-and-a-half-hour drive each way seemed daunting on a Sunday late afternoon. I took a pass. In the years that followed, I have regretted that decision. That decision was placed on a list all of us parents have who've lost kids. Things I did wrong and would do differently list. We all have them. Sometimes, they keep us up at night and sometimes, it just makes us double over in grief and regret. But those events have happened and cannot be undone. So, now what? Well, I have made peace with those decisions, and when in the right spiritual frame of mind, I even embrace them. And then every once in a while, I remember there is a God, and all things take place in his world.

How in God's name (literally) can I say that? I had an opportunity to see my boy on stage performing an act of kindness, and I stayed home. But let's look a little deeper. I, of course, had no idea that this opportunity wouldn't come again. I know I've been a good father and have gone to great lengths to be present for my boy (and still do). But I sure blew this one. But maybe, just maybe I wasn't supposed to be there. Let me explain. I have had so many wonderful experiences with Chris that have come up in so many medium readings. From golfing, to fishing, to ball games. We shot pool, shot guns, and shot the breeze. I have a catalogue of memories to draw on. Sally does not have as many. Chris and I were both guys' guys. And we did guy things. Often together. But Sally was not part of that. Because she isn't a guy. So, maybe this event on stage was supposed to be for the two of them to share. Then and for eternity. Maybe I wasn't supposed to be there. And maybe I'm letting myself off the cosmic hook. But I think it's possible and even probable that this was supposed to unfold just as it did. At least I sure hope so.

I have learned from this. Given the opportunity to golf or have lunch or just hang out with my two other kids, I jump on it. I seize the moment. I know now what I really didn't know before; each moment is precious and fleeting.

Who would have guessed I would be the guy quoting Omar Khayyám? *"Be happy for this moment. This moment is your life."*

CHAPTER EIGHTEEN:

A Good Egg

"Pete, you're a good egg."
~Billy Beane in *Money Ball*

A GOOD EGG

In the film *Money Ball*, Billy is struggling with some weighty life decisions and Pete makes him watch a film clip of an athlete overcoming adversity right on the field. A victory of the spirit that puts it all in perspective.

Billy stops before walking out the door and announces, "Pete, you're a good egg." It was a recognition, an anointing.

The movie touches me on a few levels. The first is that Chris looked like Brad Pitt. Brad captured Chris's reckless spirit in *A River Runs Through It*. And in *Money Ball*, the film, which gave me an opportunity to view what Chris might have looked and maybe even acted like in middle age. Chris too, like Billy, was a good egg.

It seems like a silly, outdated term, doesn't it? Maybe something your dad would say. But it isn't because it says it all. It takes in the whole of the person and puts them on the egg scale. They are weighed and measured. And they are or they aren't. If a person is mostly a good guy but doesn't come through… they aren't. If someone is a good egg, they just conduct themselves a certain way. Supportive, consistent, understated. They are there and they come through, every time. Good egg status is special. When you lose a kid, the true character of someone is revealed. Some people can't deal with your sorrow or intense grief. I understand that limitation. But it knocks them out of the category. They can be nice guys, or even good guys, but if they can't put aside their issues to be present, then they aren't good eggs. Take a moment and do a list. A good egg list. I'm blessed to have so many good eggs in my life. Starting with my best pals Al and Rick. Sawyer is a good egg. So is Mike C, Brad, Jeff, Paul, Aric, Jerry, Jimmy C, as well as too many friends and family members to even list. Good eggs travel cross country to attend the Chris McQ Annual Golf Outing despite hurricanes and/or COVID. They pull your kid out of sub-par hospitals despite repeated staff warnings about authorizations. Good eggs fly home from China for your kid's wake, and drive in from Michigan to handle your son's minor legal case, and then take on his friends' cases as well. All at no charge. Good eggs keep people away when you're crying in your office and dare people to require an explanation. Chris's Godfather never left my side during that horrible first week. Gordon Lightfoot wrote a song about good eggs entitled, "Rainy Day People." Good eggs just listen while you break down. I'll tell you something: If you aren't sure whether you're a good egg, you probably aren't. But you can be.

Family values have a lot to do with the kind of adults our kids become. Some parents gauge success by school grades or financial achievement. I'm not saying those things don't matter. They do. But at the end of the day, I am so grateful that my kids are both good eggs, in every sense of that magnificent term. As for me, when my nine innings on this side come to a close, and the third strike is called, I wouldn't mind people looking back and saying, "You know when all is said and done, he was a good egg." Then I will know I have done my job, and I will know my boy is proud of his dad.

CHAPTER NINETEEN:

FIND YOUR THIN PLACES

FIND YOUR THIN PLACES....

I love this phrase. The first time I heard it, it grabbed me. By the way, my thin places are very likely different than yours. Although, we may share a fondness for some of the same spots.

I first heard the term "thin places" was when I was listening to a book by John Holland (remember, I love listening to books driving in my Jeep). The term grabbed me immediately. I had experienced such places but hadn't defined them. Here is how John Holland describes them in his book, *Bridging Two Realms*:

"Have you ever experienced a particular place where you've felt closer to God, Spirit, or Heaven? You just know there's something special about that place, and it feels as though it touches your very soul.

The sense of peace and tranquility encompasses your whole being, and for some inexplicable reason you're drawn to this place, even though you don't truly know why. When you're there, it's almost as if the veil between this world and the next has been lifted, if only for a short time.

In the Celtic tradition, such places are called "Thin Places." There's a Celtic saying that Heaven and Earth are only three feet apart, but in these Thin Places, the distance is even smaller.

Thin Places not only make us feel calm but also transform us, as if we're being unmasked. While we're at these places, we're aware that we're far more than just a physical being—we feel ourselves as a spiritual being, our true essential selves: body, mind, and soul. The Thin Places can be found anywhere on the planet, including churches, temples, beautiful landscapes, and ancient ruins."

*(https://www.soulspring.org
is-there-a-special-place-that-touches-your-soul)*

He had me at *Celtic.* But my heart sang that I now had a name for the places that have brought me right next to the other side. If you've experienced a thin place, you know it. It's not subtle. I was planning on writing about thin places later in the book in chronological order. But I was prompted to sit down and do it now. Right now. These promptings, like thin places, aren't subtle. But I believe these messages are like a good spaghetti sauce. When it's ready, its ready. I have been looking forward to writing this chapter for a while. So, let's go. Let's talk about thin places.

I was brought up Catholic, and as a kid, I attended mass with my family every Sunday and on holy days. But I never felt a connection to those places. I rarely sought out chapels or churches when seeking answers. I really didn't know any better. However, having attended Catholic schools through my freshman year in college, these places were always accessible to me. Despite those years of Catholic education, I wasn't spiritually awakened. Far from it. I rebelled against the long-winded sermons and the judgement, all of which felt like an effort to control me. But keep in mind, I was a bit of an idiot. I was the youngest of ten kids. I was spoiled and self-centered. And I know what you're thinking. I'm not being hard on myself. I was a handful, and not in a good way.

So, it came to me as a surprise when a place overtook me. My first experience came to me in 1999 or 2000. Sally and I had traveled to Paris for her cousin's wedding. This was my first time visiting Paris. Hell, it was only my second time on the continent—the first time was our 1991 honeymoon in Greece. (I can use terms like that as a published author; but you can't—it would seem pretentious.) Remember, I was a blue-collar kid and only got a passport when trying to impress Sally with a trip to the Caribbean.

I was very excited to see the City of Lights. And it didn't let me down. We walked around Paris every day. We experienced the *Bateaux Mouches Cruise, took a train to Versailles, and even drove to* Giverny (the home of Monet). I actually stood on the bridge where he painted the Water Lilies. I may have been a hooligan growing up but thanks to my sister Marcia, who was able to grind off some of the rough edges, I loved poetry, Monet, and theatre. Go figure. We visited the Louvre, the Musée d'Orsay, and I ventured solo to the Musée d'Armée. I even saw Napoleon's horse, which is stuffed and on display. It's a really small horse by the way. I loved Paris, and loved the Parisians. I found that if you at least tried to communicate in their language, they were gracious and kind. I would have my morning coffee and pastries in the hotel dining room and head out to explore the neighborhoods. I would come back late morning and Sally and I would begin whatever activities she had planned out. She is a planner and I'm a wanderer. She knew the city and spoke the language. After a few outings together we agreed, or rather, I was *instructed that she would do the talking. I was allowed one phrase after messing up morning and evening greetings as well as an occasional Bon Chance. And here it is,* "l'addition s'il vous plait." I was allowed to ask for the bill, and pay it by the way. I was able to use this very same phrase while in St. Bart's with Sally. It turned out to be a pretty useful phrase.

One excursion that I was somewhat looking forward to, possibly out of Catholic Obligation or *obligation Catholique* (see, I caught on), was to Notre Dame Cathedral or *Notre-Dame de Paris*, meaning *"Our Lady of Paris."* The construction on the Cathedral began in 1160 and was completed in 1260. Generations of Parisian family members would finish their day jobs and then head to the Cathedral to voluntarily work on its construction. It was truly built with sweat and love. The stained glass was called that because there were no dyes at the time. Berries were crushed to use in the scenes requiring red. The windows can be a bit gory so they must have used a lot of berries. I found just that one fact so amazing; there were many similar facts.

I wasn't prepared for what happened next. As I walked down the aisle toward the alter, I began to weep. I mean really weep. I wasn't sure what was happening. I had approached the visit as a historical one with a little faith sprinkled in. I couldn't tell you what was moving me. But I was truly moved. Sally was surprised and maybe a little pleased that I was so spiritually moved. I couldn't really explain it and wasn't able to get my arms around the experience until later on—after Christopher had crossed over and I had been exposed to and learned about thin places. Looking back, I sure as heck had experienced one; maybe my first, and most certainly not my last.

Another visit to a thin place that only made sense in hindsight was to the St. Joan of Arc Chapel on the grounds of Marquette University in 2014. Caroline had chosen to attend Marquette and we were touring the grounds. She told me of a chapel she thought I would find both historically and spiritually interesting. She was right. The chapel is a quaint medieval structure sitting on a beautiful piece of land on the campus, in the middle of Milwaukee. The structure was rebuilt stone by stone from the original structure in France. It was previously reconstructed on Long Island and then moved to the Midwest. I was mesmerized. St. Joan had visited and prayed at the chapel on March 9, 1429 after meeting King Charles VII of France. St. Joan prayed to a statue of the Virgin Mary while standing on a flat stone which sits behind the altar today. Afterward, she knelt down and kissed the stone. Legend has it that the stone kissed by St. Joan maintains a different temperature than all the other stones around it. I can tell you it's not a legend. I prayed in the chapel and kissed the stone (which was in fact colder to the touch than the others). I was moved. My spirit was moved. I wasn't sure what it was, but there was something going on there. Something from another place. Another plane. This chapel touched my soul. The place was sacred.

Both Notre Dame and St. Joan of Arc Chapel had an effect on me. They both moved me, or as Tennessee Williams wrote in *The Glass Menagerie*, *"came upon me unawares, taking me totally by surprise." I didn't know what to do with the emotions that came over me at either spot so I just let it roll over me. I guess it was good training for dealing with the grief later on. I had unknowingly touched something just out of reach. I had no idea what or where. I didn't understand it then, but I would later.* "Life can only be understood backwards; but it must be lived forwards," wrote Soren Kierkegaard. I get this quote now. I mean I truly get it.

So, what of thin places now, since I have begun this journey back and forth from the other side? Thin places play a significant part in my journey. By now I also know that energy plays a huge role in connection and therefore communication. The thin places, whether shared by others or even the public, and the ones very personal to you, are part of your journey, too.

Here we go…

Another early encounter with a thin place was around 2000. Our family was staying at a quaint, little hotel with rooms right on the Gulf of Mexico in Naples, Florida. Things in my business life were spinning out of control. By the way, when someone says that, it never means spinning out of control in a good way. I was fearful and panicked and saying my share of foxhole prayers. One evening while I was walking on the beach, wringing my hands and repeating my new mantra "oh no, oh no" or something like that, I got a tingle on the back of my neck and felt at peace. Something shifted, but I wasn't ready to trust it. Heck, I couldn't even define it. It took a while, but things all worked out. That feeling though stayed with me. I filed it away until I felt it again sixteen years later when I was seeking out my boy, and we connected. The strongest being on two beaches in Sarasota in November of 2016. But we'll get there. I no longer believe in coincidences, and I am writing this chapter sitting on a patio overlooking the sands of Siesta Key, while the dawn breaks.

CHRISTOPHER'S BEDROOM

Chris's bedroom on Scott Avenue is a thin place of mine. It had been subsequently turned into my office after he left home. I can feel him there, I can smell him there, and in my mind, I can see him asleep in his bed with a limb or two hanging over the side. Let me clarify. I see him from memory. Although, I can actually feel his spirit, smell him, and know he's around. I will tell you that only recently while deep in meditation (at my desk in his room) at 3:00 a.m. I have begun to see him. He is sitting and then standing by a pool of water. He is tan and he's wearing a pair of off-white-colored pants or khakis, with pant legs rolled up to lower-to-mid-calf. He's wearing a white shirt, untucked cotton or possibly linen, with the sleeves rolled up to the elbow. He's sitting down by the edge of the water and then he stands as I approach. I see that beautiful sideways smile and those loving, dancing eyes. My God, how I miss that boy. So, maybe clairvoyance is beginning to creep into the repertoire.

Recently, we were doing some renovations on our home. While I was down in Florida, Sally wanted to repaint my office and change the curtains. I put my foot down—a rarity when it comes to decorative choices around the house. I want his room just as I have it. Including the Landshark surfboard suspended from the ceiling, photos of me and Chris, and clutter. Plenty of clutter. It feels like him in there. A neighbor approached me about all the work, inside and out, we were doing on the house and asked if our intention was to sell. I told her no. We were doing all the work on the home because my intention was to die there. I hope I didn't scare her. But I love our house. I walked in it for the first time in the summer of 1994 just a few months after Chris was born and knew it was for us. I bought it almost on the spot. I have raised three amazing kids there, and even during the most trying times of my life, once I was home, I felt safe. You can't replace safe. Maybe if the books become huge hits, the house will be preserved like Hemingway's home on Key West. Except without the cats. I can't stand cats.

That room, his room, is a thin place. His spirit moves feely in there. Chris came to me for the first time on January 3, 2017, at 3:00 a.m.—the same time he was crossing over to the other side exactly one year before. He continues to come to me there and promises our connection will continue until I make that journey. One I know I will not make alone. He told me so. So, I know it's true.

BEACHES AT NIGHT

Beaches at night. Specifically, Florida beaches at night. Even more specifically, Florida Gulf Beaches at night are thin places for me, for us really—Chris and me.

It started in November 2016. I was attending my best pal Allen's wedding. I love Allen like a brother, but I didn't want to go. It's a strange thing after you lose a child. You really don't want to go anywhere. Also, every amenity or luxury seems self-indulgent. Why should I be allowed to travel to Florida during a harsh Chicago winter? I couldn't even keep my son safe. It really doesn't make any sense to anyone but you. And other parents in the same situation. My friendship with Allen has spanned nearly fifty years. Jeez. But it took on a new level of closeness after Christopher crossed over in 2016. You see, Allen's beloved wife Debbie died in March of 2005. So, Al has some experience in grief and heartbreak. And I trusted Al. I trust him as much as anyone in the world. When Allen spoke to me like a brother about the way things are, and the way they would be, I listened. It's funny that a couple of trouble-making, blue-collar knuckleheads would embrace spirituality through heartbreak. But it happened. I had to attend Allen's wedding in November of 2016 because it was important to him. And he had done so much for me already. It was a new chapter in his life and new chapters are important. I attended the dinners, the cookouts, and the boat rides. Despite myself I was having fun. On the evening of Allen's and Sandy's wedding (she's a great gal), I was enjoying their friends and family all gathered to celebrate them. I got reacquainted with Allen's sister Karen and his brother-in law, Vince—I remember looking up to them as role models when we were kids. It was a lovely night. I found a number of like-minded guests at a cafe table on the sidewalk and enjoyed a fine cigar with my new pals.

The music was playing, and I could hear wine corks popping; that was my sign to hit the road. I opened the door on an Uber for a guest and headed to my rental car. It was an Irish goodbye of the finest kind.

When I got to the rental car I cut and lit a fresh cigar (sorry Avis) and turned on the GPS. I entered "beaches" and began to follow the commands. It took me to an empty beach. I believe it was Lido Beach, located on one of the barrier islands off Sarasota proper. I parked, took off my loafers, rolled up my khakis (I wasn't wearing any socks—hey, it's Florida). I began to walk on the sand, cigar in hand. There was a full moon, and its moonlight danced off the gulf. I was content. I was where I was supposed to be at that moment. As trite as it may sound, I felt at one with the universe—something at that point which was pretty rare for a restless guy. And then it happened. I felt something come over me. Like electricity traveling from my head to my feet. It was energy. And it was undeniable. At that moment, I knew Chris was with me. Standing next to me on that beach. It was a knowing. I began to talk to him. I began to cry. I wanted that moment to last until he came for me when it was my time. To this day, I get a chill when I remember that moment. That life-changing moment when I knew the truth, My Chris was with me.

The following night I ditched out of a cookout and headed for what I thought would be the same beach. But the GPS took me to another beach just south of Lido. I ended up on Siesta Key Beach. It wasn't an accident. Spirit wanted me on Siesta Key that second night. It happened again. Just like the night before. I began to cry knowing Chris was with me and he had the ability to visit when he chose, and the conditions allowed. Later on in a reading, the famous medium Thomas John told me Chris walked through me that night. When researching our first book, I found that the sand on Siesta Key isn't sand at all; rather, it's quartz crystal that flowed down and covered the beach 2,000 years ago. I keep a jar of Siesta Key sand in my office and sprinkle a little of it on the page when I'm transcribing a visit from Chris. I have also had amazing visits on Naples Beach at night. It has something to do with the water, and the sand, and the air. To be perfectly honest, the "why" is beyond me. It's above my pay grade, as my pals in the military would say. But I embrace it. I revel in it.

MARCIA'S HOME IN NAPLES, FLORIDA

I have always found joy at 224 Countryside Drive in Naples. Sally and I first visited right after it was built with our little baby Christopher in tow. This home is now and has always been a safe and loving place for us all, especially for Chris and me. It has only become one of my thin places on my current visit after Marcia had made the journey across. But Marcia's spirit and Christopher's spirit move freely and happily here. I love this place and will continue to run back here when I need to feel loved. To feel safe.

I spent almost two months at Marcia's home this winter. Working, writing, and connecting. Oh yeah, and playing an occasional round of golf. Later on, I will write about an amazing impromptu reading there. The energy there fills my soul, and I am happy there, I am content there.

THE RANCH (IN BALANCE RANCH ACADEMY IN COCHISE COUNTY, ARIZONA)

In Balance Ranch Academy is a boarding school for boys seventy-five miles south of Tucson in Cochise County, Arizona, about five miles away from Tombstone in the heart of the

Sonoran Desert. It's surrounded by the Rincon, Chiricahua, Huachuca, and Dragoon mountain ranges. The Ranch specializes in treatment of teens with addiction. My boy spent a year there as a student and then another year-plus as a staff member. He developed his spirituality there. And I believe Chris found his best self there. He would work with the teen boys on their spirituality, accountability, and their step work (as in the twelve steps of AA). He was a shining star there. I have previously written of driving back from Tucson to the Ranch to say goodbye on the same spot we would say our goodbyes when he was on this side of the veil. I go there annually to talk to the boys, to share my experience, strength, and hope, and maybe a meal with them. I walk the Ranch and feel my boy there. A part of him will always be at the Ranch. The Barrassos, who had taken him in like family, dedicated both a fire pit and a new bunk house to Chris. During my last trip there, I was leaning on a fence looking at the herd of horses. Sally texted me to find Emma, a spirited paint that had been assigned to Chris during his time at the Ranch. I asked a Ranch kid and he pointed her out in the middle of a dozen or so horses. As I ducked under the fence and started walking toward the herd, she approached me. I embraced her like an old friend, and I was both beaming, and crying. The veil doesn't get a whole lot thinner than when I am walking those grounds surrounded by those desert foothills.

SEDONA, ARIZONA

I was excited to go to Sedona and went to Arizona for the better part of a week. My plan was to fly into Phoenix, hang out with my dear friends, the Sawyers, and spend the night. The next morning, Michael (the other Uncle Mike) and I would drive to Tucson Country Club to meet my pal Steve and play a round of golf at this great desert course, and spend the night at his beautiful home set in the foothills of the Catalina Mountains. That night, all three of us would attend the annual Ranch fundraiser, Fresh Start. The proceeds of the fundraiser go directly to a scholarship for a teen boy (or boys) who needs what the Ranch provides but doesn't have the means to attend. Half of the net funds from The Chris McQ Annual Golf Outing held in September go to Fresh Start. I am honored to sit on the charity board and play a small part in the miracles they perform. Look it up, and make a donation. It's such a worthy cause. Steve attends the golf outing every year. He buys a foursome and either brings a pal or two from Tucson or fills it with local friends. He's a stand-up guy.

We attended the fundraiser and had a hoot. Because it's a southwest theme I was wearing a pair of Tony Llama Ostrich boots that still fit after all these years. Although I did have to buy a new cowboy belt. Go figure. Sawyer and I awoke early, said our goodbyes to Steve, and headed south toward the Ranch. We arrived early and walked the grounds. They gathered up the boys and I spoke to them from the heart about recovery, a higher power, and the love that's available in all their lives. And the difference the Ranch had on my boy. We were seated in a circle, maybe twenty-five boys and me. And, like every year, the boys began the talk leaning back in their chairs with arms crossed, and ending with tears and hugs and promises. My God, I love that meeting. It is truly one of the highlights of my year.

After the meeting, we kicked around the cowboy town of Tombstone, checked out the shops, and unsuccessfully attempted to sneak into a reenactment (old habits die hard). We did get to see the sight of the O.K. Coral shootout. Spoiler alert: it's not where the actual incident took place. So, we wrapped up our cowboy town visit and headed north to Tucson. We had plans to have dinner with Chris's dear friend (and ours as well) Sam

DuPont. Sam is a starving artist so spoiling him with a fine meal was a treat for me. Besides, I got to break bread with two fellas who are like family to me. Mike is like a little brother and Sam feels like a son. Although I picked up the check, I was the one being treated. I love both of those guys with all of my heart. And they loved and are still loved by Chris. After a great meal filled with love, laughter, and plenty of stories (someone once said that being Irish means, "you don't know how to tell a short story"), we headed to Phoenix for a much-needed night's sleep in the Sawyer's home.

We had an early morning tee time at a local club primarily used by members of pro sports teams coaching staff. Sawyer always, and I mean always, has a local hook-up. After a fun round, I jumped in my rental and headed north to Sedona. I have read extensively about Sedona being a seriously spiritual spot. The amazing energy supposedly came from a combination of being on Indian land and the surrounding mountains being on shifting plates. The latter part was over my head as science was never my forte, despite Father Joe's best efforts at St. Francis High School. But I had previously booked a Spirit Tour of the Vortex, and I was ready to be moved.

The Sedona Visitor Center describes a vortex like this:

"Sedona vortexes (the proper grammatical form 'vortices' is rarely used) are thought to be swirling centers of energy that are conducive to healing, meditation and self-exploration. These are places where the earth seems especially alive with energy. Many people feel inspired, recharged or uplifted after visiting a vortex."

There is something there, I mean really, there. But I think my expectations were so high I just couldn't get it. The woman I booked for the tour was the perfect guide. She was an old hippie who moved west from Buffalo, New York a lifetime ago. She was an amazing character. I really do encourage anyone booking a tour to stay away from the canned tours given by lads dressed like they're in a Crocodile Dundee movie, complete with Aussie hats. My guide was the real deal. Halfway through the tour (which she ended up extending by a full hour), she set up a medicine wheel on Sacred Indian land. We went through the stations, and she told me Chris had been with us since the beginning of the tour. She explained she was a medium but didn't practice mediumship since her tour service kept her busy. I wasn't that surprised when she told me she saw Chris, and he had been around me since I had started the tour. You meet the nicest people on sacred Indian Land.

Although I felt something around the vortex I can't say I was taken by the place. I was actually a little disappointed. However, at the very end of the tour, the guide asked me to stand atop of a hill and hold my arms up. She took a picture that looks like me holding up the sun. The real prize at the bottom of this Cracker Jack box was a blue-green orb below my feet in the picture. That orb is the same color as the eye on my Christopher cardinal tattoo on my right forearm. I had been very particular about the color of the bird's eye to match Christopher's. Maybe I'm reaching. I don't know a lot about photography, but it sure seemed to fit the mood. The energy. You decide for yourself.

The vortex was a thin place. And maybe I'm spoiled by such amazing past events. But I expected more. However, it's kind of reaffirming that all thin places don't fit one size. Someone else may go to the vortex and be moved beyond description. It just wasn't the case for me.

LILY DALE

Lily Dale is a hamlet, connected with the Spiritualist movement, located in the Town of Pomfret on the east side of Cassadaga Lake, next to the Village of Cassadaga. Located in southwestern New York State, it is one hour southwest of Buffalo, halfway to the Pennsylvania border.

I first heard of Lily Dale during my sophomore year of college at Fredonia State. My friend was telling me about her mom who was a medium at Lily Dale. She was a bit sheepish discussing it as it was 1976 and society had not yet embraced the metaphysical. But I thought it cool and interesting and that was that. For some reason, I assumed the spiritual enclave was up in the Catskills, where Rip van Winkle came from.

A couple of years after Chris's transition, our friends the Fitzpatricks hosted a dinner for us and the Nyes. Sally and I don't socialize much. I never did and since we lost Chris, Sally has lost her desire or tolerance for small talk. However, the Fitz's and Nyes are dear, dear friends who like us, have no tolerance for social horse hockey. My book (our book) *My Search...* had just come out and I believe I brought a few copies to the house. We were discussing the afterlife, when Paul related a story about an impromptu visit to Lily Dale. Paul, like Brad, is a brilliant musician and a beautiful guy, and a wonderful part of my journey. He was in Western New York on a work trip and a conference for the day was cancelled. He had heard about the spiritualist community nearby, went to check it out, and decided to get a medium reading. During the session, his cousin came through who had been killed a few years prior in a car accident. His cousin spoke of his beloved car. Paul knew exactly the car and the accident. Paul said there were a number of undeniable facts validating it was his cousin. Paul then told us about a documentary called, No One Dies in Lily Dale.

I asked Paul exactly where it was. He told me it was in Western New York about an hour south of Buffalo. Near a town called Fredonia. Well, hello... I spent my sophomore year right there. Lily Dale was fifteen minutes from Fredonia State and about forty-five minutes from where I was raised. I had to check this out. I went home and watched the documentary and began to hatch a plan to get to Lily Dale.

As I mentioned earlier, we always travel to Crystal Beach, Ontario, the first week of August for the annual McQuillen family reunion. My plan was to spend a night or two in Lily Dale and then do a book signing in Buffalo, before heading up to Canada the next day. Because I always drove, changes in plans were never a big deal. I usually drove with one or two of the kids, and sometimes one of their friends. Because of Will's lacrosse schedule, he and Sally usually drove separately a few days later. This also gave Sally the ability to leave Canada a little early if the mood struck her (after Christopher had drowned). You always need an escape plan.

This year, Caroline chose to come with me. We had planned to stay two days in Lily Dale but a TV interview with WKBW TV in Buffalo came up, so we shortened it to one. I had done a little research and discovered all the houses in this enclave were owned by mediums. Each practicing medium had to undergo rigorous testing to be certified as a Lily Dale medium. This was as legit as it can get. I booked a room for us at a bed and breakfast (actually no breakfast) called the "Jewel of the Lake" and scheduled a reading for both Caroline and myself with the owner Teresa. The place was beautiful. It was a gated hamlet on the shores of Lake Cassadaga. We arrived in the morning to a lot filled with vehicles that had license plates from all over the country. We walked the grounds and checked out the little shops selling books, crystals, sage, and incense. There were a few small coffee shops and a restaurant. There was a meeting hall, and the homes of the mediums lined the streets. It was really pretty cool. A whole community dedicated to spiritualism and metaphysics operating since the turn of the last century.

Wikipedia offers this description:

Lily Dale was incorporated in 1879 as Cassadaga Lake Free Association, a camp and meeting place for Spiritualists and Freethinkers. The name was changed to The City of Light in 1903 and finally to Lily Dale Assembly in 1906.

After our little community tour, we checked into our room at the Jewel, meaning we dumped our duffle bags into a room with twin beds. This is the kind of place that kept that old-world feel including a lack of amenities. But we weren't there for a spa atmosphere; we sought the mediums and the connection. We met Teresa on the front porch and confirmed our sessions later that afternoon. We had discovered there was a gathering at Inspiration Stump twice a day where mediums address the crowd and perform random readings. Inspiration Stump was originally used as a stage for the orators but is now preserved as a bit of a shrine. The crowds are seated on wooden benches in a clearing and the mediums are up front near the stump.

The Lily Dale website describes Inspiration Stump as follows:

"Inspiration Stump is a retreat found at the end of a quiet trail of the Leolyn Woods. It is not unusual to become aware of the spiritual energies while in an open and receptive state at the Stump. Demonstrations of mediumship are presented twice daily at 1:00 PM and 5:30 PM. This tradition dates back the establishment of Lily Dale in 1879. Mediums have been holding services at the site affectionately known as "The Inspiration Stump" which was named after a sacred pine that once grew there."

Caroline and I attended the 1:00 p.m. session, and we were joined by Kathy Zillner, my old friend from high school. It was so nice to see her after all these years. One time back in high school, she thwarted an unwanted advance by hitting me on the head with a cork-bottomed Dr. Scholl's sandal (ouch!). It never happened again. But through Facebook she had learned about and read my (our) book. Kathy had been a frequent visitor to

Lily Dale over the years and a student of the metaphysics and she volunteered to be our guide. The session was impressive but since I had already been in the presence of some amazing mediums, I was far from overwhelmed. But it was pretty cool. We ventured back to the Jewel for our afternoon sessions. Caroline went first and I made myself scarce. Her reading was her business, but she did share most of it with me and it was accurate. Then I had my turn. It was spot-on. Very specific. Undeniably coming through was Chris, along with Sally's dad Warren, and my uncle Bill and brother Bill, my mom, my dad, and my brother Jerry. I will cover it in more detail in Book 3. "Hail, hail the gangs all there," Teresa said. And she said she heard the song, "When the Saints Go Marching In" playing, which I had mentioned previously was our family song, and the processional song playing as we exited Chris's funeral. I mean there it is.

As I'm writing this chapter, I'm listening to the Lily Dale medium session I had stored on my iPhone. If you ever venture to Lily Dale, or visit a medium, I really encourage you to tape every session. There is no way you can retain from memory what goes on, and you don't want to be distracted from the messages by scribbling notes. What I do is record the sessions then listen while transcribing them on a legal pad later.

The session was an hour. And it was full of wonder. I can't help but think the grounds were just flat-out conducive to spirit communication. Maybe because the path was worn down by a century of spirit visits. But we will get to worn-down paths shortly.

After my reading, I took a walk and ended up on a dock overlooking the lake. It's not surprising that I found myself sitting on a dock near the lake to process it all. I am drawn to bodies of water, much more so after Chris's transition. Here is how Intuitive Medium David Hanzel explains this connection to water:

"If asked, I offer you this theory. Going back to the beginning of this story, it was said that water could take on the energy of a person. Water brings life, whether from this world or maybe the other side. We are attracted to water because it has a life force." That makes sense. A life force is energy—all energy. After a quiet time, Caroline and I walked the little hamlet and settled into the one restaurant on the grounds for dinner. What continued to strike me about Lily Dale is how serene the place actually felt. It was in the air. People came from all over the world to experience what Lily Dale had to offer. Everyone was happy and everyone was kind. It is really a good place in the best sense of the word. We had left Chicago at 3:00 a.m. that morning and we were physically and emotionally spent. We had a big day ahead. I had an interview with a hometown TV station during the afternoon and a book signing in the evening. So, I should have been preparing for a good night's sleep. But I had a plan. One that didn't include a full night's sleep. My plan was to go to Inspiration Stump at 3:00 a.m. and see if I could connect with Chris on those hollowed grounds.

The alarm woke me at 2:45 a.m. As quietly as I could, I got dressed and moved downstairs. It was dark, I mean the kind of dark you get in the woods—dark. I grabbed a flashlight from my Jeep and headed toward Leolyn Woods. I had to admit I was a little on edge. As I walked through the woods en route to Inspiration Stump, I felt an electricity. Of course, I was walking through strange woods in the middle of the night, but it was more than that. I really felt a charge in the air and around me. When I passed the Pet Cemetery it was electric, and as I headed toward Inspiration Stump I could feel an energy coming from all around me. As if all the souls who come to connect with the earthbound were sending vibes. It was an amazing experience.

If I had ever had doubts that places could hold energy imprints of the souls that had inhabited or do inhabit them, they were dashed that morning. I made it to the stump and sat down. I placed a recorder on the stump hoping to catch an EVP (electronic voice phenomena). But when I listened later all I heard was the rustling of the leaves. However, I was far from disappointed. Believe it or not, the electricity had died down as I sat in the clearing of Inspiration Stump. It was peaceful and calm. And I meditated. After a bit, I headed back through the woods and felt the same electricity on my return trip. There was a sense that I was a welcomed visitor, but the place belonged to the souls. Lots of them. I was only passing through.

After being a little let down by my experience in Sedona, I was trying not to have very high expectations about Lily Dale. But the place knocked me off my feet. It is truly a spiritual enclave where we can share in the spirit world. If I were looking for a thin place, Lily Dale would certainly be high on my list of places to visit.

SACRED HEART CEMETERY

Sacred Heart Cemetery is a thin place, specifically around Grave #9, Lot #15, Block #32, Section 3.

Not to be confused with Grave #10 where Chris was originally buried, before we moved him one plot north. I have told this story already. But I actually believe all the effort makes this setting perfect. All that energy helps to make this one of my favorite places on this planet. It's gorgeous, quiet, and open twenty-four hours. It's a wonderful spot where Chris and I can be together. I take pride in keeping his grave neat and clean, and standing tall. It says someone loved is here. Even though he's not always there. But you get it. I have received signs there and felt him around. I sit in a chair and look out through the woods, or lay on the grass and look up at the sky. We meet his friends there and we cry there. It's probably the reason I will never move from Winnetka. That and his bedroom which we have discussed. This section of Sacred Heart is a place where Chris and I meet. I can have a cigar and just be. Just the way we would when he was on this side. I can feel him, hear him, and smell him here. I come here sometimes just to try to stop the world from spinning. I'm not sure a place can get much thinner than this.

I was very much looking forward to writing this chapter on thin places. And while some places are shared spots, like Lily Dale, Sedona, and Siesta Key, others are for you and spirit. Like at Chris's grave in Sacred Heart Cemetery.

Literature has made reference to thin places but by other names. Read the novel *The Shack*, by William P. Young, as well as The Razor's Edge, by William Somerset Maugham. Maugham swears that the events in India were autobiographical. The focal point of both of those books are in fact, thin places.

I really encourage you to roll up your sleeves and find your thin place, or places. It may take some effort or planning, or the place or places may take you completely by surprise. But it's a big deal. It can truly be a game changer. A life changer.

CHAPTER TWENTY:

THAT'S WHAT FAMILY DOES

In February 2013, my beloved niece Kerry died of a brain aneurism. She was a shining light of love to all in the family. She left an adoring husband, and two wonderful boys adopted from Korea. They had gone to Korea to adopt Ryan six years before and Alex joined the family a few years later. They were six and two when their mom transitioned. Kerry was forty-three years old. Her kids really needed her. It just wasn't fair! I have subsequently learned that fair is where you go to ride the merry go round and eat cotton candy. Fair doesn't count, it doesn't figure into anything. But Kerry had died. The whole family came in from all around the country to console each other and say goodbye.

After the wake, the funeral, the internment, and the reception, we Chicago McQs went back to the hotel to get ready for our flight. Chris had been living in Vermont and working with the DuPont brothers. Sam and Zack were like family and both brilliant musicians. Both before and after Chris had transitioned, they would stay with us when touring the Midwest. They loved my boy, and we sure love them. Sam called me the day after Christopher drowned and said how sorry he was he couldn't attend the service. But as a struggling musician it wasn't in the cards. He asked me what he could do for me, for us, and I asked him to write a song. A day or two later, Sam texted me a song he wrote and performed entitled "Stay Put." It's on sound cloud. Or follow this link: https://soundcloud.com/tributetochrismcquillen. You should listen to it. No one has ever given me a sweeter gift and I love Sam.

"STAY PUT"

Spoke to you the other day it was quiet and you were gone. Asked a couple questions about where you are and where you've gone. To tell you that your Daddy called and asked me to write a song. About a son of his too sensitive for the world and all its faults.

I just called to say I know you're doing well you're driving 'round with us today. I can hear these stones, your heart is always stronger than the places you have gone.

Truth be told I always knew you were a better friend than I. Reckless as a hurricane tunnels in your eyes.

Refused to have a bad time when you rolled up out of bed. And I'd be pressed to find a soul who can't admire the way you live.

I just called to say, cheer up and carry on I'm shining down on you today. I can hear these stones, you stay put. Cuz you're just where you ought to be.

So, Chris had come in for the funeral from Vermont, where he was staying and working with the DuPonts. As we were packing to go home, Chris informed me of his decision to stay in Buffalo. He wasn't asking for my permission. But I guess I raised him that way. He told me he overheard that the Buffalo family was scrambling trying to find a temporary fix before a permanent solution could be figured out for child-care. Kerry's husband Bill had to get back to the business he and Kerry had formed. He had two little boys to provide for. And everyone else in the family also had to get back to jobs and lives. "Dad, I've decided to stay on and help with the boys until Bill can figure it out." I was moved and concerned. I told Chris I felt it was a monstrous responsibility, even temporarily. I may have even tried to talk him out of it. "That's what family does" my oldest responded, "that's what you taught us."

Here was my nineteen-year-old boy schooling me on family commitment. I was still concerned but now beaming with pride. I raised my kids to be part of a clan. And my son was showing me what that looked like. Chris stayed for two months. He changed diapers, made meals, drove to preschool, and stood up. He did the job with love and commitment. He nicknamed Alex, the baby, who was a small kid at the time, "Big Al" and Alex beamed. To this day, the family calls him "Big Al," and when I hear it, I can't help but smile. And sometimes, I turn away to hide my tears.

This act of love still fills me with pride. And I guess, it was no surprise that numerous mediums have told me Kerry greeted Chris when he crossed over. I was told Chris said, "Kerry, what are you doing here?" when he found himself on the other side. I'm learning, really learning that the only really important thing is love.

I got my bell rung

This past March, Sally and I were having dinner at a little spot on Siesta Key. We started talking about all of the Florida beach vacations we've had over the years. We laughed at how relentless Chris was about this activity or that. Just relaxing on the beach was not our boy's cup of tea. I was thinking back, laughing while relating a story about when I took both boys to Fort Myers Beach in 2009. Caroline was at a Catholic school and her spring break did not correspond with the boys' break. We were staying at a great spot on the north side of the island. We had a beach, a pool, and lots of sand to walk, run, or throw a football on (of course, we had a football with us). They had upgraded us to a suite and each boy had his own room. However, they both slept on the half-moon couch in the living room. Just thinking of them sleeping quietly together both breaks my heart and makes me smile. Only a parent who has lost a child can really grasp the meaning of that sentence.

We explored, had dinners, and went fishing. Those experiences were special, and the fishing was reported by my medium pal Sheri Jewel as a fond memory for Chris. But any down time was out of the question. If there was a gap in the activity, the boys would want to drive off the island to play mini golf. If I wanted any beach time it would have to be before they woke up. I had visited Fort Myers Beach during my current trip to Florida. And I drove past the marina, hotel, and Smokin' Oyster Brewery restaurant that we loved so, and has become a McQ family favorite. Sitting in that little restaurant relating all this to Sally I began to cry, I mean flat-out weep. I told her I wanted a rewind, one week. Heck, I would settle for one day or one hour. Sally didn't ask the obvious. She didn't ask, "Are you ok?" She didn't ask because she knows the answer. Because she lives the answer. But we finished our dinner lost in our memories and started walking to Siesta Key Beach to try and catch the sunset. The day before, we found ourselves on Lido Key and watched that day's magnificent sunset. It was energy, nature, Source, and God. It was, and is, Christopher. It was, and is, all of it combined. It takes my breath away, it breaks my heart, and it gives me hope.

When we got back to the condo, I went down to the beach to launch a Chinese lantern from the Siesta Key sands while Sally watched from the balcony. I was alone. Well, not quite. I

CHAPTER TWENTY: THAT'S WHAT FAMILY DOES

felt my boy around me. I launched the lantern and watched it climb high into the sky. Someone had left a beach chair on the sand. So, I sat in the chair and watched that lantern sail out of sight. It was beautiful and again like so many events, it also broke my heart. I've said it before, but it bears repeating. Anyone who says, "time heals all wounds" has never lost a kid.

Just follow the breadcrumbs and you will be ok.

Trust me on this. Whether you are trying to find your own spiritual path, or just make it through the day, rely on spirit and follow the signs.

This quote from the book *The Secret* has served me well.

Think of a car driving through the night. The headlights only go a hundred or two hundred feet forward, and you can make it all the way from California to New York driving through the dark, because all you have to see is the next two hundred feet. And that's how life tends to unfold before us. If we just trust that the next two hundred feet will unfold after that, and the next two hundred feet will unfold after that, your life will keep unfolding. And it will eventually get you to the destination of whatever it is you truly want, because you want it.

Sometimes, we are headed somewhere and end up somewhere else. Sometimes, I was headed somewhere and ended up somewhere else. I had to learn to listen to that inner voice and follow the headlights.

I remember one Wednesday about seventeen or eighteen years ago, the day that was designated as my day off. I meant to only work a few hours and be home by noon and take Chris and Caroline to Lambs Farm. Lambs Farm is a petting zoo with some amusement rides that is staffed by and for the benefit of the residents who have downs syndrome. It's a great place. As usual, I didn't check the hours of operation on this day. But remember, this was before smart phones or personal laptops. The kids and I pulled into the parking lot expecting soon to be riding on a miniature train and feeding a goat or two. But as we parked it became clear the farm was closing. My two little kids, who moments before were laughing excitedly, went to into disappointment mode. I thought I could do both that day. But what does the Bible say about serving two masters? I hadn't been listening. But I needed to do something. The day wasn't going to end this way. I backed the truck out and headed north on I-94 toward Wisconsin.

"Where are we going? What's going on? Are we going home?" were the shouts that were emanating from the back seat. Twenty minutes later, we were turning into the parking lot of Great America, the Midwest's premier amusement park, complete with giant roller coasters and superhero theme rides. The sky was the limit. We hit all the rides, had burgers and ice cream, and reveled in the day. It was fantastic. Even after nearly twenty years, I can sit back in my chair and smile remembering that day, after I wipe away a few tears (maybe more than a few).

We were heading squarely into our own personal iceberg that late afternoon, but instead ended up with an outing and memory of epic proportions (is that dramatic enough for you?). I don't think that day would have had the same impact if we had started for and arrived at Great America as our initial destination. Luckily, I followed an inner voice that day. I wasn't trusting the process then. I didn't know about the process, I hadn't read *The Secret,* and I sure hadn't learned to really turn it over. But somehow, I followed the road in front of me and the result was a day of pure joy, and a memory I can wrap my arms around and recall when I'm feeling blue.

My time on this planet isn't yet over. And following the headlights now is how I travel. It's how my life is unfolding, how I roll, about two hundred feet at a time.

THE NEXT TWO HUNDRED FEET

It's real time now and I have been in Florida staying at my sister Marcia's home in Naples for just over a month. It's an amazing spot. This has been a favorite place for me since she had moved here twenty-seven years before. It is light, airy, breezy, and safe. I was always loved here. It was a favorite place of my Christopher's as well for all the same reasons. His Aunt Marcia (his Godmother) adored him. She loved him, and she never held back that love. I came here to escape the cold of a Midwest February and to escape the chaos of a renovation at our home in Winnetka. I came here to recharge after a hectic year in the mortgage business. And I came here to write.

To experience, feel, and write.

Coming here was a great idea. I drove down on February 1, stopping en route in Nashville to visit with Sally's brother Ricky and his family at their new home in the south. I continued my journey arriving in Naples, Florida on Sunday after too many cigars, Red Bulls, and just the right number of audible books. When I arrived, I was greeted by my terrific nephew Michael and his wife Trish. They were wrapping up their own visit to Casa Feeney (Marcia's married name) and stayed an extra day to have dinner and play golf with their Uncle Joey. It's what the kids all call me. Joey is what the family calls me and that comes into play in a bit. Hold your horses. My nephew Michael is only about a half decade younger than me, being my eldest brother's oldest child. Michael has a special spot in my heart as he has attended every one of the Chris McQ Annual Golf Outings, always with one, two, or last year all three of his adult boys in tow. Because of COVID, he drove over from Virginia, with one of the boys, spending the night in Indiana, picking up another boy at Midway Airport on Chicago's south side, then driving to O'Hare to pick up the third boy, and continuing on to Glen Flora for a noon lunch and 1:00 p.m. tee time.

My Christopher had been joined at the hip at any family event with Michael's twin boys Matthew and David. Having those guys, all four of those guys, in attendance at every facet of the weekend fills my heart with joy. And I know it made my brother Jerry beam with pride from heaven. It's all about family and you taught them well Jerry. The visit with Michael and Trish was short, but warm and so much appreciated by me. While in

Nashville, I also stopped by the Vanderbilt dorms to say hello to their daughter Claire. That ten-minute visit in the dorm parking lot filled my heart. Just looking back at it makes me smile. By the way reader, if you are ever traveling and are thinking of stopping to visit a friend or especially a family member, don't think, just do it. When the visit is over and that loving feeling washes over you, drop me a line to thank me.

After Michael and Trish left, I picked up Caroline at the Fort Myers airport for a short three-day visit. We ate at waterside restaurants, hung out, and played golf (yeah, she got the golf bug as well). February 6 was the second anniversary of Marcia's crossing and I was so pleased to be able to spend time at her grave on that day. She is interred in a wall in the back of St. Peter the Apostle Church in Naples. On the way, we had stopped at a florist for a single pink rose. One that met with Caroline's approval. We placed it next to her plaque in the wall and we sat and prayed and visited.

CHAPTER TWENTY-ONE:

WHY GO TO A MEDIUM?

If you can connect... then why go to a medium? I get that question often. Since I can connect with Chris, why would I go through the time, expense, and even possible disappointment by going through a medium? It's a good question and I want to validate it. But it's crystal clear to me (get it?) that each source of connection has its place. To me, it's like going to a restaurant for a meal you could make at home. To me, the answer is that the food is better because the prep and actual cooking is done by a pro. And chefs, like mediums, have varying skill levels. And like a chef, if the product isn't good, you most likely don't go back. I have had readings with mediums who seemed to flat-out miss the mark. That happens. A lot of energy and chemistry go into a reading. Like mixing fire and ice. (I've been waiting for an opportunity to use that line... it works, right?) I believe the medium has to be able to connect with a spirit and the spirit has to want to connect with the medium. It may sound a little crazy but remember, we are talking about communicating with souls who have transitioned.

However, I also think personality has something to do with a quality reading. For example, my medium friend Sheri Jewel is brash, outgoing, a little crazy, and very sweet. She has become an amazing medium. She has two kids of her own. Her son is my boy Will's age, and they actually know each other through friends. She understands boys. She gets them. Rambunctious boys grew up in and around her house, and experienced her love and when necessary, her wrath. But she gets them, and they get her. Like I do. Therefore, it's no surprise that Chris is so very comfortable with her. He comes through her all the time. I've grown to expect that when Sheri and I are chatting on the phone, Chris will most likely pop in. I love the term "rambunctious boys." It's a title to a John Fogarty song. Early in their lives I had attached a song to each of my kids. And "Rambunctious Boy" was Chris's. It's a song very close to my heart. Hey, you may even have a rambunctious boy in your life. On this side or the other. Why not take a time-out and listen to the song? It may make you smile. I'm going to take my own advice and do the same.

I am not a medium. I have been told by mediums that I am intuitive. Ok, I'll buy that. And that in itself is such an amazing gift. But just like me scrambling eggs at home or going out for a fine meal, the results are going to be much different. That's why I rely on mediums. I want the one-on-one connections I get with Chris. But I also want the dynamic connection that comes from someone who has honed their skills to facilitate a strong, direct connection with someone on the other side.

What follows is a good example of why I so value mediums and their skills, and quite often, their generosity of spirit. This happened a few days ago.

Just this year on March 3, I was sitting on the lanai patio at my sister's house in Naples. The third of the month is always a tough day for me, because it's Chris's anniversary. I had made it through the day and was enjoying a beautiful summer like evening and a good cigar. It occurred to me, or more accurately the thought was given to me, to call Sheri, my medium pal. I could tell she was happy to hear from me and that made me feel good.

I told her about my stay in Florida at Marcia's house and Siesta Key and the current events surrounding my southern sojourn. (Remember, as an author I'm allowed to use such phrases.)

We spoke of kids, and friends, and events. After a bit, I asked her if Chris was around her. He usually comes through, and his presence is announced to her by a tingling around her head. I heard her call out once and then again. Christopher, are you here? And then nothing. My heart sank. Truth be told, it was a bit of a crappy day anyway. You can have those even in paradise. I mean Florida, not heaven. But then Sheri responded that another spirit was coming through. She told me it was my sister Marcia. Marcia told Sheri, "Thank God he straightened out." She was referring to my wild youth. She told Sheri there were times when she was concerned I would die early. Marcia was worried about my drinking and recklessness. She had also gone through the horrible experience of dealing with a sibling's suicide. I did, too, but I mostly dealt with it with alcohol and outrageous behavior.

Sheri said she mentioned a sports jacket and thought it was a Bears jacket (God forbid). It was a Buffalo Bills jacket that Marcia had given Chris on that last Christmas on this side. He absolutely loved that jacket. This jacket has come up in a number of readings since his transition. Sally wears it occasionally and we keep it in the closet in my office. We cherish that jacket, and I am grateful he didn't wear it on that fateful weekend. Rather, he wore my Buffalo Bisons baseball jacket. He had it on in the photos I had to identify at the scene. Just recounting that moment brings tears to my eyes and makes me want to throw up. So, if you have a similar reaction to a memory, please just let yourself feel it. It will pass. Not the love or the heartbreak. But the nausea passes. That Bisons jacket sits in the coat closet at home. I tried to wear it to a hockey game once, but I came back inside and returned it to the closet. I can still be a bit of a basket case.

Marcia showed Sheri a piano and that made me laugh. Let me explain. When I moved to the D.C. area, where Marcia was working and raising her kids, we would all go to Mr. Smith's, a well-known piano bar. There was one in Georgetown and one in Tyson's Corner. When family came in or for occasions such as birthdays we would all meet there. By sheer numbers and will-fulness, we would invariably take over the piano bar. Attending patrons would either join the fun or fade away. It was a ball. Drinks would flow and songs were sung and laughs were shared. It was so much fun. It really was our place.

Well, on to the rest of this amazing reading. Marcia told Sheri she was happy I was in her home. Sheri asked if I had put flowers on Marcia's grave recently. Which we did of course on the second anniversary of her crossing just a month before. Sheri asked about a seashell. Like a silver dollar shell. I had just returned from a week on Siesta Key where Sally would walk the beach and bring back a perfect set of shells for her collection. I brought back one. And just that morning I had picked it up and put it atop the driftwood-framed picture of a cardinal I had sent Marcia on a previous Christmas. So, that's incredible. But it gets better. Sheri asked about a family photo. On a bookcase about three feet away from the cardinal picture is a framed photo of all ten McQuillen kids taken in maybe 1961. It was actually a professional photo portrait. And it somehow really represents us. It's our family photo.

Marcia told Sheri she wants to be in the book more. Well, you got it, Marcia. She wanted me to know she is with the brothers and other family members on the other side. And of course, she is with Chris. Marcia asked about a ring. For Christmas, I had ordered a ring for William with the McQuillen crest on it. The same crest is tattooed on both of my boys' biceps. The ring had arrived late. So, I brought it with me and gave it to him when he visited his Aunt Marcia's house just the week before. He loved it. Of course, he did. Like all of us he loves anything McQuillen.

Sheri then told me Chris popped in. She said he was so full of love but did have a dark side. A sad side. She said he had a higher purpose. She said he lived on the edge and took risks. Sheri said Chris knew he was going early. "Pop, you know how I was. I was deep and introspective."

He was a mixture, she said. Chris told Sheri that seeing the work I'm doing on the second book makes him very proud. "Stop doubting me Pop." Chris told Sheri that he stands behind me. Especially when I write. He told her he was with me when I was crying today. Which I was.

Marcia now came back and mentioned Checkers. But not the game. She was referring to a bar named Checkers on Hertel Avenue in Buffalo, New York. Marcia and I would go there and drink pitchers of sangria when I was going off to college. Sheri said Marcia's energy was maternal. Almost like I was her little boy. That was true. I was five years old when Marcia got married and I was her ring bearer. She said her love for me was like a parent. Like my love for Chris.

Marcia told Sheri to ask me about her house keys. When I left for Siesta Key, I put them in a designated spot. And when I went to look for them, they weren't there. The cleaning guy must not have returned them. No big deal. But Marcia warned me not to get locked out. So, I walked into the kitchen and took the main set of keys off the hook on the wall and put them in my pocket. I then returned to the lanai, all the while talking to Sheri, who was talking to Marcia and Chris. Get it? Sheri then informed me that Marcia said, "Put the keys back on the hook." What? That's friggin' amazing. So, I walked back into the kitchen and did what I was told. But how you do ever question a connection when something like that happens in real time?

Marcia closed the visit by telling me her home is my home. And I always felt that way. And she said, "I love you Joey." "Did she call you Joey?" Sheri asked. Yeah absolutely. She called me Joey. This is why I value my relationship with mediums. They are special. They have a gift. One given by Source and one honed to an amazing level. Their job is both rewarding and heartbreaking. They have added a level of connection for me to the other side that I never could have achieved on my own. God Bless them. I truly mean that.

ON OCTOBER 5, 2018 CHRIS VISITED.

Hi Dad,

Not a lot of room for me. You are full of fear, regret, anxiety. Clear that out and I can fill the space. Trust it. Trust me. Feel the tingle on the back of your neck. It's me. Work hard, trust more. I know you are getting back in my world. But if you want to be close, don't stray so far. OK, all good. I love you forever & I'm always here for you. You don't need to dial in. I sent you a sign with the first meditation. Just write it down & see OK? I know you are trying to expand, but as Shari Elman told you, I'm not a show-off. Under the radar. The cardinal was not a mistake. Signs will keep reinforcing it. I'm progressing over here but I'm still your boy. That's for all time. Honest. See the cardinal in the meditation? You get it now don't you? Back in the flow Pop. Here we go. That's what faith is. Not all proof, right? You have to decide. But you know. So knock it off. I do love you so much. You gave me complete love all the time. Sometimes I didn't think I deserved it. But I now know love isn't earned. It just is. Keep attending lectures and meetings. You don't have it yet Pop. You're not that smart. Not a shot. But it will take a lifetime on your side to get your arms around it. Then you go. Then you come to me.

What a day that will be Pop. You & me again. No fear, or anxiety,
or depression. Just love. Feel it. I'm sending it. Hey Pop. Lean back.
About friggin' time. "Live Like You Were Dying." You sing it. Now
live it until you cross. Way to get back. Now I'm happy. Now I'm
proud of you. You clearly feel lighter don't you? Because you were
starting to doubt. Holy Crap. How could you doubt? Stay with me
Pop. Don't doubt or lose focus. I love you and that's the payoff.

Yeah Dad. I remember Minnesota. Part of me was already
leaving but I didn't know it. It's a plan. But you can't fathom it
till you cross, then it will all come. Aha, get it, and I'll be smiling
at you as it sinks in. That's it. You'll say, No shit.

We're back you and me. So don't pull away again, I can't
do it all. You have to pull your weight. Your substantial weight :)
Like a flood gate right? You should feel lighter. Your spirit is lighter.
Your soul is lighter.

Remember when we ate sushi in Old Tucson then Fogo? I
loved being with you Pop. It's OK. It's all OK. How can this be so
intense but light? That's the trick. That's us, on your side and more.

Good start Pop. Now go to bed.
I love you
Chris

Chris gets right to the point. For us to connect, I mean really
connect, I have to be in the right frame of mind and spirit. The
fear and anxiety can dampen the connection. It clutters up the
field. I need to stay close and focus on what's important. He's
reinforcing that he sent me signs in the meditation.

He talks about not being a show-off. During a medium
session with Shari Elman, the medium from The Well, I asked
about leaving a recorder for an EVP. Chris told me that wasn't
his style. He's not a show-off. Lots of lessons for the old man in

this visit. He talks about Minnesota. I traveled to St. Paul the summer before he transitioned to bring him his Jeep. We had a great time. We golfed, shopped, ate well, and went to a St. Paul Saints minor league baseball game. I bought him a Saints ball cap that he loved and wore constantly. He's wearing it backward on the cover of *My Search*... But I did feel something was missing with our connection, then. And in hindsight, I believe he was already starting to move on from this earth plain. Or as Craig McMahon calls it, *Earth school.*

To cheer me up, I think he brings up Old Scottsdale and mistakenly calls it Old Tucson. That validates that they're not perfect over there. Just evolving. When he mentions Fogo, he's referring to Fogo de Chão Brazilian Steakhouse. Remembering that trip brings me comfort. He does that. He comforts me and calms me down. A couple of weeks before he transitioned, Caroline was involved in a car accident and although we got it all handled, I was still worked up. It was a Sunday, and I went upstairs to watch the Bills game. Chris came up and laid on the bed next to me like he used to do when he was a kid. We just hung out and watched the game. Even at that moment, I felt it was a special moment. I just didn't know then how special.

When things get tough, I lean back and remember that day. And guess what? It may make me sad, but it calms me down and I know we will do it again. Thanks for that, Chris.

OCTOBER 16, 2018

Hi Dad,

Enjoy the meditation but I'm already here. Been waiting for you. What you're doing is the most important thing on your agenda. Enjoy the moment. Love the moment. It's us. It's me. So very proud

*of you. Proud of me too. You know I guided you. I know you trusted
me in the process. Hang on, the ride is going to be fun. You & me
just the way we always wanted it. The cover should be the most
real one. You know the one. Because we are the most real together.
All around you now. We're all pulling for you on this side. I sent
you Lisa. She feels me guiding her too. Can't go wrong. You stayed
on point Pop. Good job. Organize Book 2. It will take a while but
that's ok. I'm around Caroline, she will open up more this weekend.*

*I loved that day in St. Paul. But part of me was already
moving on to a new life. No way for you to know. I didn't. But you
couldn't take me home because I was preparing for a new home.
You felt something. But you couldn't put your finger on it. It was
over your head. Above your pay grade. But you've caught up. Lots
more to learn. But you are learning to learn. That's a key to a lot.
Learn how to open us to messages. Writing, feeling, and eventually
seeing. I promise Dad, it's in the cards.*

*I miss you too Dad. We will share this place. This incredible
place. It will be like crossing a shallow stream. You have to cross
it yourself. But I'm right on the other side. So, it's just natural to
walk across to me. And then you're in. You'll be on the other side.
You & me. How's this for awesome? But not today. Today is for
writing books and presentations. Carry the word Pop. We are all
behind you. Jerry says Hi. Jerry said he loves you and he's never
been more proud. He now understands the struggles you went through
& loves you more. He's a good guy Dad. Cardinal, cardinal, cardinal, cardinal. Keep the symbol up front. I'm content Pop. Like
the picture on the cover. I was right where I wanted to be & that's
now for me. You're getting there, not just yet. Glad you are pursuing
the mediums. Keep the personalities out of it.*

*Sleeping in Old Scottsdale. Waking up in a bed next to you. It
was safe, so safe. When I went out on my own, I lost that safety.
Didn't know how to ask for it. It's a choice but also a path. Hard*

to understand right now what that means. But it means I'm with you right now & I love you. Keep that Dad. Keep that close.

I'm beautiful now Pop. Really am. But it's still me & you. I was never ashamed to love you Pop. You were the rock. You were my home. I loved that hat Pop. I loved that day. We are together now, but later on just like before. But better. Don't worry about the body and how it works. Just trust me. It's ten times better than you could ever guess. Ever imagine. To you I'm still the body, the form of Chris. It's how you'll see me so don't get caught up in it. Just accept.

I know you are sorry Dad, but all I remember is the love. Thanks for that Pop. But it's not necessary. You loved me with all your heart and that's as good as you could possibly do. I know you miss me Dad. I'm sorry I had to leave. But that isn't going to change so you need to accept it. Embrace it. Make peace with it. I'm happy. If that's what you always wanted for me then I'm there. I'm around, but you need a push. I'm behind you now Pop. Pushing you, guiding you. How do you think you get away with those close calls? Rental car in reverse. Yeah, that's right. So, say thanks more Pop. It's me. Feel the weight fall off. You took a full breath.

I love the book and the focus. Talk less about it. It will speak for itself. Smile & know Pop. It's all me and you. Don't forget you Dad. She'll be fine Dad. Caroline will be fine, I promise to step in and help. Did you see the moon? Well so did I. We share the same moon Pop. Sounds like a song. Leaving is hard for you tonight Pop. Because it's so close between us. Look for a cardinal today. Not proof. You don't need proof. Just a sign. Just a smile from your boy.

I love you Dad
Pulling back
Chris

So, I've been connecting with Chris and keeping one foot in the other side for a while now. But this visit was a bit overwhelming even for me. It's all amazing but he actually tells me what it will be like for me when I cross over. When I transition. "It will be like crossing a shallow stream." I mean, I can picture it in my head. The woods, the rocks, and the stream. What a gift he gave me. And you. He tells me I have to make that step from this side to the other on my own. But he is on the other side waiting. Holy cow! Now I know. Now you know. But he also tells me that as appealing as it all sounds, it's not my time yet. This time is for writing books and presentations. I get it.

He tells me Jerry says Hi. Jerry transitioned in 2014. My brother Jerry was an amazing guy. He was a hero of mine and he was larger than life. He was a man among men. Everyone always wanted to be around Jerry. From Jerry, I learned a lot about how a man conducts himself. Remember, I was his baby brother who could do no wrong. But in my twenties, I was wrapped in my addiction and running amuck. Jerry was always there to literally and figuratively bail me out. Maybe my biggest shame was that I knew I was letting Jerry down. But with God's love I was able to turn my life around.

Fast-forward to 2001. The family was attending a wedding in Tampa. I had over a decade of sobriety and had achieved a modicum of success in the business world. As was my custom, I would bring one of the kids with me to a family event. Wedding, retirement party, etcetera, and seven-year-old Chris was with me this weekend. One night, the McQuillen family had a big dinner at a local marina. It was beautiful. We were surrounded by water, with the stars twinkling above. It was really a fun dinner. As the meal wore on it was time to settle up the bill. Jerry was at the head of the table, and I was on the far side. He signaled the waiter and then caught my eye. With his forefinger, Jerry pointed to himself and then me. Indicating we would split the bill. I was flushed with pride. Jerry was showing his total acceptance and even indicating we were peers by bringing me into the select few he would split a large dinner bill with. It's funny, isn't it? Years later at Jerry's funeral, after I went to bed, Chris split the bar bill with one of his cousins, because as he said, "Dad, that's what you would do." And he was right. Because that's what Jerry would have done. I love my family and I love Jerry. Chris telling me that Jerry is proud of me makes me flush again with pride. Almost as much as that evening in Tampa. Almost.

Chris talks about Old Scottsdale. I woke up in the bed next to Chris watching him sleep, keeping him safe, and doing my job. I think it's common for those of us who've lost kids to think deep down we've failed them. Failed in our most important job. But he tells me it's a path. He also lets me know he's around and helping. He's helping me. Something about a rental car in reverse is an example. I don't remember it, but I'll take his word for it. He is also looking out for his family. He lets me know cardinals are indeed signs. Not coincidences. He makes me laugh. I was thinking, when I cross, I want to see, I mean literally see, my beautiful twenty-one-year-old boy with the sideways smile. If we are energy, then how would it work? In this visit, I get my answer. Don't worry about it. I'm still the same form. Ok, got it. He tells me we share the same moon. I love that. I mean, I really love that. Because I do look up and say goodnight to him. We share the same moon. Sounds like a song, doesn't it? Let me get together with Brad and see if we can get that done.

This time of year, the fall season, is tough on us—those of us who have lost kids. Halloween kicks off the upcoming holidays. Lots of colorful costumes, lots of noise, and lots of joy. It makes me smile and it hurts like hell. Please be gentle with yourselves, especially now.

READING WITH SHERI JEWEL OCTOBER 30, 2018

Upon review, it sure seemed like a pretty busy time for me with mediums and such. Maybe it's the upcoming Halloween or maybe it's just the way it is. But on October 30, I had a session with Sheri Jewel. She started off by telling me Chris takes full responsibility for the events that caused his drowning. "Dad," he said, "don't worry about it." Sheri said he was showing my heart. Chris says he feels like he's making a difference in the world. There was purpose to his life. Chris tells her he is using me as a vehicle. It's God's plan. I'm supposed to be telling stories. He says that every step of the way I shouldn't doubt. Sheri said he's showing her a big smile. And saying people were drawn to him.

Chris starts talking about our family, the McQuillen family. He mentions esophageal cancer. That's what eventually took my brother, his Uncle Jerry, a year-and-a half before Chris joined him. Sheri says he's showing my mom. She mentions crossword puzzles and an apron. My mom says I "put her through the wringer." Which was so true and just the way she would say it. That's a term she would use. More accurately, that's a term she did use. My mom said she is very proud of me for making something out of myself. And she told Sheri that I did have a temper. Spoiled kids often do (that was from me, not my mom). Mom said there were other family members on my side. Sheri tells me Chris is present with my mom but he's letting her talk.

Sheri asked if I knew somebody who crossed at forty-nine years of age. She said she is being shown a sports car, and said he's in a better place. Holy cow. Sheri was talking about my brother Billy who was killed in a crash in a sports car in 1993 at the age of forty-nine. Billy says he is also taking care of Chris and that Chris was greeted by family. Sheri said Billy was talking about someone daring him to do a sled hill. Ok, now this takes the cake. Here is the story behind that statement.

When we were kids on Clifton Parkway, in Hamburg, New York (a suburb of Buffalo) we were at an unofficial toboggan/sled hill. It was a nice, gradual, if not bumpy hill down toward the beach. Both Jerry and Billy came to join us. Jerry had had a few snowy runs in already when Billy showed up. Jerry pointed not to the well-worn toboggan run but rather to a steep hill, made of shale, complete with rocks and trees heading straight down to a creek. The implication was that we were all doing that run. Which was absolutely not true, but typical of Jerry. And Billy being Billy, reckless and free-spirited, grabbed a sled and jumped on it, heading downhill toward a very predicable crash. Which in fact happened. We all watched in horror as Billy crashed off one tree and then another and the sled exploded under him leaving only two twisted metal runners and some kindling. When he emerged from the snow crash looking like the abominable snowman, but unhurt, we all looked at Jerry. "Jeez," said Jerry a bit sheepishly, "I thought he knew I was only kidding." This true story has been told at many a McQuillen dinner table or cocktail hour, and now it's been shared by Billy on the other side. I mean, you absolutely, positively, cannot make this stuff up.

Sheri told me she saw that Billy lived life the way he wanted. And he apologized for leaving this world so abruptly. He takes full responsibility for his death.

Sheri then said she was hearing from another spirit. She said, "Tic Toc Grandfather." That was amazing (again) but my goodness. Sally's grandfather Tony Michel died in 1998 at the age of ninety-two. Prior to his crossing, "Bompa" as he was known by family had written his memoirs, *Tic Toc from Grandfather's Clock*. Sheri said his spirit is around. She described him as very dignified, proud. Although a model of integrity and etiquette, he did occasionally take a drink, she tells us. See, here is where the conspiracy theorist hit a wall. There is no way to connect me and Chris to Sally's grandfather. Sally's maiden name is Stearns, and the memoir was printed and distributed to family only. It was never published. Plus, she described him to a T: he was dignified and proud, with integrity and etiquette. If you knew him, you would know those are perfect terms to describe him. And he did in fact enjoy a cocktail or two. I remember fondly visiting Bompa and Nanny in their lakefront condo when Chris was just a baby. Bompa kept some toys in a closet for Chris—toys from another generation but they did the trick, especially the locomotive that Chris would play with. When Chris was born in April of 1994, Bompa and Nanny were still wintering in Florida. We have a photo of Bompa, sitting in a chair dressed in tie and vest, holding Chris for the first time. His first great grandchild. He and Nanny, Sally's grandmother, were lovely people. And Nanny will come through later on to her beloved namesake, Sally.

Christopher tells Sheri I am going to write another book. I will get some info in my dreams and it will be a bit of a roller coaster. Chris is mentioning pictures of fishing, which he said is in the book.

So, here are some points of validation from Chris. He mentions a memory blanket made out of his T-shirts, which in fact his mom had made, and I use often while sitting in my chair watching TV. He mentions a family crest, which is the tattoo that he and Will share. He mentions his initials on a tattoo. His initials are on Will's tattoo and I have CJM on the tattoo of a cardinal on my forearm. No, I'm not a St. Louis fan, but Chris sends me cardinals as signs.

Chris says he's "Sorry it happened, and I am the best dad ever." He mentions a jersey with his name on it. On the wall of my office below the Landshark surfboard is a Buffalo Bills jersey, with Chris's name sewn on back. It has the signature of every member of the AKL fraternity on it. It is beautifully framed and was given to me by the AKL boys in the spring of 2016. I look at it every day as I write. He talks in depth about his sister. He wishes he was a better brother on this side. He says he's trying on the other side. But I say this with all sincerity, that is their story—Chris and Caroline's. It's comforting to know he will always be there for her.

Sheri is telling me Chris's transition left a huge impact on his friends, Will and Caroline's friend, and lots of people. We are all picking up the broken pieces. Chris touched a lot of hearts.

Sheri is telling me Chris wants to ensure the second book is not redundant. It has to be "fresh" he says. He wants me to know he's never going away. Always at my side. He tells Sheri nothing can tear us a part. When you die, Sheri says, "He'll greet you."

Sheri is reporting that a Labrador (Casey) is Chris's best friend. He tells her, "My pals are with me too." He says, "The kids are all ok, hanging together. They're sorry for their families, but everyone made peace with their decisions." He specifically mentions Patrick.

He tells Sheri he is like a camp counselor on the other side, making the kids happy and helping with their transition.

Sheri remarks that Chris is just special. Chris tells Sheri that if we move, he will move with me. No plans right now, but good to know. He says, "Tell dad I love him, and I'll never forget him." Sheri says I showed him love which wasn't always easy (yes it was). He says that as a kid, he hates that he put me through trauma.

He tells Sheri, "That's all for now. I'll talk to you later." Chris says he's "always by my side in the car." She says his soul touches you.

Ok, so to go through this line by line would be insulting to you. Chris makes himself very clear. He had so many validations.

By the way, how could this book not be fresh when all the data comes from Chris? Chris on the other side. It would be hard to dull that subject down. Thanks, Chris. Just reading these notes as I transcribe them leaves me in a state of wonder. And hope, and love.

NOVEMBER 4, 2018

Hi Dad,

Lots of contact lately. Failing is a good thing. It speeds up the intro process like a well-worn path. I can come through easier because I know. You will also someday. You will be able to temporarily cross over to my side, our side, and then come back. Lots of thought and words on this astral travel. But it's just coming over and back. Safe. Well, the book is coming Pop it's you and me, just the way we like it. Go with it. Flow with it. I didn't say go with the flow. Too glib. I'm here Pop. See me sitting in the golf cart in St. Paul. Every moment of that trip is on a slide show that I can look at. So is Florida, so is Christmas. All spring breaks and all Christmases. Every decision made by you to help me. Please know I love you, and even the wrong ones were still from love. Try to keep peace. I'm good Dad. I know your heart. I can look right into your heart now. So much love for me. So much love. Walking out the door to the rental car in the Buffalo Airport. You made me feel warm and loved. You were love for me. Thank you. You're on the path Pop. I'm never far from you. It's going to sink in. Keep trying.

I brought the family with Thomas. He's a good guy Pop. It was so much fun. I love being a McQ and I love being your son on this side even more. Besides I can look into your heart. Let it all go. You are on a new path. A writer's path, an intuitive path. (I'd say empath, but let's not push it.) There will be a next book. Just

keep walking forward like you always did. It will present itself.
Love my dog. She will be with me soon enough. She's pure love, and
will love it here. Like heaven. Never mind it is heaven.

Organize tomorrow and get #2 on track. I'm with you Pop.
Every step of the way. Give Teresa my love. She's so good for you Pop.

Always and all ways.
Chris
PS 7:30 a.m. Tell Teresa, Jerry says Hi!

There were 375 words in that visit. It amazes me that Chris could
pass on so much in so few words. But it's really consistent with
who he was, and apparently, who he is. And there is something
magic about the story inside this story. But I'll get there. I will tell
you that if you are on the path, you need to keep notes. Because
if you don't, something important in your story may slip through
the cracks. You'll see what I mean.

My notes tell me I awoke right around 3:00 a.m. and fell back
asleep. I got up at 4:00 a.m. and tried to play catch-up. Chris
came through. No harm, no foul. But it happens. Sometimes I try
to get up when I know Chris wants to connect and I just cannot
make the gate. I awake a few hours later, guilty and a bit hung
dog. But Chris doesn't seem to mind. We get there when we get
there. And I'm always relieved that he's ok with my human failings.

Chris talks about astral travel. Actually, I wrote it down as
astro travel. But that's not a thing, well actually it's George Jetson's
dog, though that doesn't really matter. But I thought you should
know. He talks about our weekend in St. Paul, and says it's on a
slide show he can recall whenever he wants. That's comforting.
Something else that's interesting is that he makes reference to
me picking him up at the Buffalo Airport in a rental car. I always
drove from Chicago to Buffalo, and then on to Canada for our

annual family reunion. I know that. But what I think is really enlightening is that he made a mistake. The memory wasn't about the vehicle, it was about the contact. That first glance that warms the heart. But I write what I'm told and wrote rental car. Now, when my niece Kerry died, I did pick him up at the airport in a rental car. Maybe he's referring to that. But I mostly remember picking him up as he walked out the doors wheeling his golf clubs with a duffle bag over his shoulder. My God, seeing him made my heart sing.

He made reference to Teresa. That's my cousin Teresa. She was one of the younger cousins. I used to raise hell with her older brothers. I reunited with Teresa at my brother Jerry's funeral. There was something very special about her spirit. A few years later, she was coming into Chicago with her kids to attend a hockey tourney for their youngest boy Paul. We all spent the day together and went to dinner. Caroline, of course, chose the restaurant and became the tour guide. We bonded as family. I attended a few games of the tourney and really felt connected to my cousin and her wonderful family. Her boy Paul feels much more like a nephew to me than a third cousin and I treat him that way. But this connection all came through my brother Jerry. He really loved Teresa and I think wanted me to take up the mantle of supporting uncle when he crossed. I did, and I get much more out of the relationship than anyone else. So, at the end of the visit, Chris is making reference to family, and says, "Give Teresa my love."

When I awoke at 7:00 a.m. there was a follow-up message from Chris. "Teresa, Jerry says Hi."

Holy cow.

Here is the part about keeping notes or recordings. Chris slipped in that he brought the McQs to Thomas. That triggered a memory and I pulled out my notes. On October 27, just a week before, Sally and I decided to attend a "Night with Spirit" with Thomas John, just a few towns away. I had received an email about the event a few days before and Sally and I decided to make a date of it. Besides, there is a good BBQ restaurant a few blocks away. Hey BBQ and spirit—sounds like a good combo.

The event was being held at the Infinity Center, in Highland Park. There were maybe 100 to 125 seats and it was at capacity. We arrived early and grabbed front-row seats. Thomas came in and explained his gift and then jumped right into reading the audience. He was truly amazing. He was just nailing it. A woman who had kept her maid-of-honor's dress who had died of an overdose before the wedding. A trip together to Vegas, before her death. A brother, a mother, and on and on. He was like a gatling gun. Most of his attention was to the left side of the room, and I began regretting my choice of seats. As Thomas did his thing, I kept noticing him glancing off to his far right. All the way to the left of us. He was nodding and acknowledging a presence.

He would then go back to reading his audience on this side. But he was obviously being interrupted by guests we couldn't see. And he decided to give up the goat and address them. Thomas looked over the audience and stated that there were a number of family members from one family coming through. And the numbers were increasing. "Frankly," Thomas said, "they kind of scare me." He laughed.

That's when Sally elbowed me and told me she was certain it was my family. I could tell she was hoping we wouldn't get in trouble for my family crashing the event and scaring Thomas. But I knew he was kidding. At least I think he was kidding. Anyway, he decided to address the crew pushing through the veil. "Ok," said Thomas, "who has a big family on the other side and one member's name is Jerry? But his name is a variation of Jerry and it's not Gerald." Another elbow from my wife caused me to raise my hand. Thomas wanted to know the spirit's name that was leading this pack of hooligans. "It's Jeremiah," I said. That's my oldest brother Jerry. He said Jerry was accompanied by Billy, Kerry, Pat, and a brother who took his own life in the mid-seventies. That was Bobby. He asked if Aunt Pat got teased and lovingly made fun of. She did. He said there was a young man behind her throwing bunny ears behind her head. He asked me if that was my son. As he had a son's energy. I told him it was. He told us Jerry led the troupe but is now backing off so Chris can come through to send his love. This was amazing. Chris was smiling, Thomas said, and that he's the best-looking spirit in the room. He told us what a loving and advanced spirit Chris was.

Thomas said that before he left, Chris wanted to bring through a young man who was very shy and wasn't comfortable coming forward. Thomas said it was as if Chris had his arm around the boy and was bringing him forward to connect with his mom. Thomas mentioned both names and the mother stood up. She said her teen son who had died recently was indeed very shy. The young man just wanted his mom to know he loved her and was always around her. The rest is their story. But Thomas told the woman she should thank Chris for bringing her boy forward. And she did just that. That was vintage Chris for sure.

Before he moved on, Thomas looked at me and Sally and asked, "Who's Sarah?" I pointed to my wife Sally next to me and Thomas dismissed it. (Sally is a nickname of Sarah.) "No," he said. "Sarah, on the other side, who is 100 years old." My wife Sally responded that it was her beloved grandmother whom she was named after who did indeed pass at 100 years of age. "She doesn't say much," said Thomas. "But she loves you and is always around you." Sally so welcomed that message from her beloved Nanny. And just like that, Thomas moved on.

A few days later, Ryan Bailey (who goes by Bailey), one of Christopher's best friends, came upon a photo of himself and Chris and forwarded it to us. In the picture, Chris was behind Bailey and throwing up bunny ears behind his head. My goodness, the hits just keep coming. You just can't make this stuff up. Have I said that before?

Not long after this, I was given a half-hour phone session with Thomas. I know what you're thinking but there is no way for a medium or celebrity or anybody that presents in large groups and has numerous daily calls with people to retain the substance of those previous encounters. I deal with a lot of people every day, and nowhere near what a guy like Thomas does, and I can't even keep names straight. Besides, the extent of what is covered in a one-on-one call is so much deeper than a group drive-by at a presentation. So, put away your notepads Nancy Drew. It's real.

Because this was on the phone, recording it becomes a bit tricky. You cannot record a cell phone conversation on the phone. So, the phone conversation was held on speaker while I recorded it on a digital recorder. Thomas was aware I was recording the session and I would be concerned with a medium who had an issue with the session being recorded.

Thomas asked how I wanted the reading to go. And as usual, I like the medium to go where spirit takes them and then save a few minutes at the end for a couple of questions. Just a funny note, I have used this format previously and usually the questions are answered in the reading before the Q&A. Hmmm.

So, here we go. Thomas said two spirits are coming through, a younger male, who "is your son" and an older man coming through in a supporting role. I commented that it was my son and my dad. Thomas corrected me and said the older man wasn't my dad but rather my mom's brother. That's my Uncle Bill. He told Thomas that he'd been wanting to come through.

Thomas asked if we had a special connection and I said we did.

Let me explain or rather describe Uncle Bill. This may take a while, but Uncle Bill is worth it. Everyone should have an Uncle Bill in their life. My Uncle Bill was a gorgeous man. Dark, curly hair and a beautiful smile. He was built like an athlete. Which he was. Uncle Bill was a semi-pro football player. The local press dubbed him, "Mighty Might, the little ball of fire." And after a few cocktails, he would regale us with stories from those glory days. He was also an amateur boxer, but I don't think he was given a nickname for those endeavors. He looked like Dean Martin, and he was a snappy dresser and a decorated war hero in the Pacific Theatre in WWII. Uncle Bill was also a railroader like so many of us in the family. And he was so cool. He loved to have a good time. He could croon a song or take over a dance floor.

And he would drink martinis. The ones in the stem glasses. My God, was he smooth. And he was tough as nails and took no guff from any man. But everyone loved Uncle Bill. And he was sweet and loving. He adored his sister (my mom) and looked up to my dad as an older brother. Although it was way before my time, he was engaged to the love of his life in his twenties, and she died of leukemia before they were married. My older brothers and sisters remembered her so fondly. I was trying to remember her name and my first instinct was to text Marcia and ask her. Funny, right? That happens. In the moment, we forget they aren't on our side anymore. Here is an example of that very thing.

A few years ago, or maybe more than a few, I was watching my boy Will play lacrosse in a local tournament. It was on Halloween and the weather was nasty. Sleet, rain, and wind. I remember Will breaking through and approaching the goalie. Two defenders boxed him out from taking a shot. He reversed and took a shot behind his back, literally backward. The goal went in, and the home-town crowd roared. I was so excited and so proud. I grabbed my cell to call my brother Jerry to tell him about it. The only problem is that Jerry had crossed over four-and-a-half months before. So, I put my phone back and just described it to the heavens. I knew he was watching. I know this has happened to you. And you should follow your instincts to connect.

But back to Uncle Bill. He eventually married a little later in life to a woman who couldn't have children. Although Bill adored her, she was a little high maintenance, and she required time and attention which took Uncle Bill away from us.

So, here is what just happened as I'm writing this chapter. The name Joy or Joyce popped in my head. That was Uncle Bill's fiancée in his early years. I know where that came from—thanks, Marcia! So, Uncle Bill coming through was a real treat for me. I know he loved me, and he loved that I played high school football. At a very young age, he nicknamed me Moose. No one else ever called me that and that was just fine with me. Because it was something between us. Just Uncle Bill and me. Another tradition I got to experience was that when we turned eighteen years old, the legal drinking age back then, Uncle Bill would take us out to a fine restaurant, for dinner and cocktails. I remember the restaurant but not much of the evening. The restaurant was the Cloister—the home of Mark Twain when he lived in Buffalo. I was eating steak (a rarity) and drinking Manhattans (a bad idea) and this is the reason much of the evening escapes me. But it was a coming-of-age moment and almost five decades later, I still look back on the evening and smile. Because they never had kids and they had two incomes, Uncle Bill and Aunt Bee would travel to exotic places like Florida and Acapulco. They would come back after those month-long vacations, and we would sit mesmerized by the travel tales. You would have thought they had traveled to the moon and back. For blue-collar kids, Acapulco might as well have been the moon to us.

So, that's my intro to Uncle Bill who was coming through. Later in my journey to Lily Dale, Uncle Bill came through again. Thomas said he had the feeling that we were from a very big family, but Uncle Bill felt we had a special connection, and I was grateful and again flattered.

Thomas said the younger male had crossed more recently and that his crossing was abrupt. He asked about Michael, who had helped me a lot during Chris's passing. That was Christopher's Godfather Michael. Thomas asked if we bought more graves than needed when I bought Christopher's. This made me laugh on the recording. Michael and I bought all the remaining graves in a row, in the mostly sold-out cemetery. We each took three graves. Chris was originally on the end of the row. He was buried in January and when the snow melted, I noticed he was placed next to another couple. That just wouldn't do, so I moved Chris one plot over and I will take the one that he was temporarily occupying. I wrestled with the decision. Was I being silly? Did it really matter? I wasn't. And it did. It mattered a lot. I go to Chris's grave often and the location is perfect. I was urged by spirit to move him, and I did. I have never for one minute regretted the decision. I am at peace at his grave. I followed that inner voice. Thomas asked if it was Chris's nature to tease or bust my stones. I said it was. Thomas said Chris was making fun of me for buying all of those graves. He's laughing about it.

Thomas asked if there were a large number of people at Chris's funeral. I told him it was standing room-only at the church and that there were 2,000 people at his wake. Thomas said Chris was showing him that. He said that Chris was showing me presenting to groups in the following years. Speaking to parents and helping people. Speaking in front of various-sized groups. Chris is telling me I need to help others. Specifically, fathers. Chris is saying, "Dad, you gotta help these guys."

Thomas circled back to the day Chris died and asked if when he was missing, did the group of people not know until much later that he was gone. And that was true. Chris and his friends paddled out on the lake around 3:00 a.m. but the other kids in the house didn't know they were missing until around 8:00 a.m. Thomas said he sees people coming to or waking up and wondering where they were. Thomas asks if Chris mentions how he has moved up on the other side. Which of course he has. He even makes reference to the earth, water, and fire levels at the Ranch. He told Thomas he's on the fast track.

Thomas asked me about a connection to September 11, the date. He said Chris circled it. I missed it during the reading and Thomas moved on. But in hindsight, that is always the weekend of the Chris McQ Annual Golf Outing.

Thomas asked about inspired writing or automatic writing. I told him about the book and our visits. He got it. He asked if it was me or Chris who was the golfer. I told him it was something we shared. He asked about a spirit named Joe, who was an older Joe. Chris told him "Big Joe is here." I said that was my dad. Thomas said he saw him with dark-framed glasses, which was spot on. Thomas said he was a very loving, committed father, but he was also a tough guy. He was so very loving yet his nickname on the railroad was Iron Joe. This nickname was imparted on him by railroaders, who were also a pretty tough bunch. So, to Thomas' question: Yes and yes.

Thomas now was back with Chris and said he was talking about Ryan and Alex. This knocked me off my chair. These were my great nephews, who Chris had taken care of after their mom's passing. The previous week, I had sent Ryan and

Alex nine pints of ice cream from a local ice cream shop. The sweet gesture may have been a bit self-serving as the family sent me a video where Alex stated I was still his favorite uncle from the uncle/aunt category. Fearing my sister Debbie would do something to change his ranking, I sent nine pints to "Big Al" to share with his siblings. The beau geste hit the mark and I retained the title of #1. By the way, I originally wrote "gesture" but, as I wrote this sentence, the term 'beau geste' popped in my head. That was a message from my dad, as *Beau Geste*, starring Gary Cooper, was a favorite movie of my dad's and mine, despite being made in 1939.

Thomas said he saw a red jersey with an Indian head on the front. This was a Chicago Blackhawks home jersey (sweater if you are a Canadian). Chris loved Blackhawks games and all his friends would of course wear jerseys when gathering to watch or attend games. The Christmas before his crossing, I gave Chris a white away jersey with the captain, Jonathan Toews' name on the back. I keep it in the closet in my office.

Thomas continued that Chris was making references to "the kids." "So, he must have siblings, right?" Thomas queried. Thomas said Chris was teasing and asking how did I get so lucky to get Mom? Chris mentioned being sent away to the Ranch and Thomas asked me, "Who's Betsy?" Thomas said to tell Betsy thank you. Betsy Barrasso was co-owner of In Balance Ranch, where we sent Chris. She was also the person who made the decision to accept him into the program after Chris was completing wilderness, despite the Ranch being at capacity. She told me on the phone that, "The Ranch would be good for Chris, and Chris would be good for the Ranch." How right she was. The McQuillen family continues their close relationship with the Barrassos and the Ranch to this day.

Chris told Thomas that I go to his grave. Sometimes at night.

Chris thinks that's funny and Thomas said I should continue
the practice. Thomas asked me about a maple leaf. At first, my
mind went to an NHL logo. But that wasn't it. Just recently,
Sally sent me a photo of Chris and me together, when he was
eight or nine years old. I looked at the shirt he was wearing, and
it had a maple leaf on it, with Niagara Falls printed across the
logo. But it could also be the beach chair. When I to the grave,
I always have a folding chair. You know, a beach chair. For the
first few years, it was a maroon chair with a white maple leaf on
it. I had picked it up in Canada, and always kept it in the back
of my Jeep for our visits. Well, I've since worn out that chair
and a Buffalo Bills chair. I'm on Bills chair number two, this
second one sent by someone anonymously through Amazon.
Thomas continued that Chris is saying that I sit at the grave,
with a cigar. Thomas asks me about a golden dog or golden
retriever. I tell him it's Cassidy. Our yellow Lab. That dog just
adored Chris and would always want to be around him. When
Chris was home recovering from a thirty-foot fall down a mine
shaft, Cassidy never left his side. And after Chris's transition,
she stayed glued to Sally. No wonder Chris used dogs' love and
loyalty to explain angels to me.

Thomas brought up the subject of Caroline and discussed
her struggles at pretty great length. He was spot-on about it all.
That's her story for her to tell. But I know Chris continued to
guide her and brought her through a tough time. It's so hard on
the siblings. She has walked into the light and continues to grow
in all ways. She is a walking miracle, and her dad so loves her.

Thomas then came to the final part, the Q & A.

I asked Thomas about Sally, his mom. That very morning
Sally was resigning her position as a staff therapist at a treatment
center to begin her own practice. Chris told Thomas it was a
good move and that he will open doors for her. Chris said the

practice will be big and a very good thing for her. Flash-forward a couple years and her practice is booming and at capacity. She has a gift for helping others, and I know how proud Chris is of her.

Thomas asked me if I knew about the "love letters." I told her we both wrote them to him when he was at the Ranch. Thomas said he was referring to his mom. I then recalled that when Chris was born, Sally wrote him a love letter and had other moms do the same. To maybe share one day in a book. Aha moment here. By the way, it had nothing to do with me. A direct connection to his momma.

Thomas asked me about a connection to Harvard. So, guess who's coming to dinner? (1960s movie). But I knew Sally's father was making an appearance. Thomas asked if he wasn't a very good dad or grandfather. Warren, Sally's dad, had acknowledged he wasn't involved in the grandkids'—my kids'—life. He wasn't. Warren did, through Thomas at a small group session, make amends to Sally. But he does pop in on readings pretty often. Even when it's just me. Funny, right? It's not up to me who comes through. I asked about the first book, which was set to be published not long after the reading. Chris said my part was done and to be patient. He was on it. It would take time to pick up some momentum. But it would happen.

I told Thomas I feel Chris and sense him, but I don't see him. How can I get to clairvoyance? Thomas said I just need to keep working on my connection. He said Chris was laughing and saying, "Dad, you take what you get."

Thomas and I exchanged pleasantries at the end. I reminded him I had recently seen him at Infinity and that the big family that came through was mine. He chuckled as he thought back. Was yours the spirit family that just kept building through the evening? He asked. Yeah, I said, that was my family. He said my older brother and my son kept gathering troupes to ensure they would get acknowledged. Yup, just the McQuillens, having it their way... even from the other side.

I went into great depth with you about this session. It was amazing. I've used that term fifty-two times so far in this book. But it is the perfect word. No other word even comes close. And anyway, it's my book. Well, our book. I wanted you, the reader, with me as Thomas channeled my son. To see the accuracy, to feel Chris's humor and hear him name names and cite events—not close-calls or almost-likes, but exact names and exact events. Remember, all this dialogue took place in forty-three minutes. It was scheduled as a thirty-minute session and Thomas just kept going. That's a pretty intense half-hour. This guy has a special gift. I am always in awe of his ability to connect with the other side. You don't need me to explain it, or help you connect the dots. It was right there. From the other side through Thomas, to me. Gratefully to me.

CHAPTER TWENTY-TWO:

A RETURN TO SIESTA KEY

NOVEMBER 14, 2018

Hi Dad,

I don't feel like talking today. Just want to hang… remember we could do this & we still can. Just love.
See the picture. That's how content I am. You can be too.

Work on it.
Love
Chris

Man, he says a lot in a very short message. He just wants to hang without talking. Like we sometimes did. So, that's just what we did. The picture of him in a hotel bed in Old Scottsdale, safe and content brings me to tears. I love him so much. But he tells me if I stay on the path, I can be as content as he was in the photo. As content as he is on the other side. Ok, I'm in, buddy.

NOVEMBER 22, 2018

Too Many Distractions

Hi Dad,

I've got to follow the path. You can't control everything. My crossing should have made that clear. Just go along on the ride. Smooth and clean like a canoe. (Sorry, I know that's not your favorite but it's a good depiction.) I know you love me. Me too Dad. I want the book to send my love and light the way. It's going to be less about you and more about service, kindness, and love.

I'm here next to you in the Jeep, going to Eagle River or Scottsdale. I'm on your right side. Relaxing and loving my dad. It's funny because you are relieved I came through today. Like I would let you down. We are one, Pop. Soul family. One soul, two spirits figuring it out. The book is really about to erupt. Don't lose sight of the purpose. Helping and loving. Good job and I can feel you letting go as you write. I love that picture and loved that day. That weekend in Old Scottsdale. The first time I tried sushi, and the AA meeting in the mall. And Fogo of course. We went there just because I wanted to. That's how much you loved me. That and a million little ways Pop. I'm smiling at you. Can you see it?

Just because you wrote a book doesn't mean you are done learning. So much more. That's the next book. And the next one. That is what you will do now. Don't you get it? Time to start writing again. The first one is now on the way, picking up momentum all on its own. Or at least without you. You will feel lighter after this today. Let go the thought of control or responsibility. Did you hear that everything is happening as it should? I've been visiting you. Now it's time for you to visit me. I picked the meditation for that reason. Don't get too comfy Pop. You're not an expert. Just an observer. There's that chill. That's me. Despite the stiff neck. How many people get to see heaven Pop? I'm showing you it. Take it in. Looks a lot like the beach in Mexico with the beach bungalows right? Well, that's your heaven. Mine too. Sort of... mine has girls, yours doesn't.

"Perhaps at this time you have found what you sought" from the meditation.

What a great visit. I love how he refers to us as being one and soul family. It's reassuring. That weekend in Old Scottsdale holds a special place in my memory bank and heart. I was back in Scottsdale last year, walking around, retracing some of our steps. I passed the sushi restaurant and the hospital he (we) stayed in a few years later after his mine-shaft incident. I even drove around the Giants spring training stadium where we took in games. I believe people become connected to places, and I'm connected to Old Scottsdale. The picture above says it all. I know I have shown it to you before, but it is part of his message. He was warm, comfortable, and safe. God only knows I wish I could have kept him that way. He lets me know he's around. Reinforcing that in case I start to doubt. He supports me like a son. Like a son and a best friend. He also reminds me what heaven will be like. He keeps my ego in check by letting me know that I'm no expert. Boy is that ever true.

RETURN TO SIESTA KEY

December 3, 2018

I was in Naples, Florida spending time with my precious sister Marcia, whose time of transition was at hand (she would take that journey a few months later). The veil was very thin around her, which was enhanced by the connection she felt with my boy Chris, who had pledged to greet her. Because I was returning home the next day, I thought I would try to connect with Chris on a beach in Naples just a few miles away. So, after a day in the hospital and a take-out Chinese dinner with my nephew Norm, I headed to the beach. I do this at night, always at night.

I arrived at the beach, kicked off my shoes, grabbed a seat in the sand, and lit a cigar. I could feel Chris all around me. The sand, the moon, and the water all bringing his spirit close. While sitting there bathed in spirit, I felt this compelling urge to head up to Siesta Key where I felt him so strongly back in November 2016. The pull to go was fierce. I had tried to get back there last year when a work call derailed my plan. But it would have been during the day anyhow, which isn't our deal.

When I was leaving Naples Beach, I wanted to ensure the trip would not be for naught and thought I should check on beach access. The internet said *Open 24 hours*. So, after a brief stop at Marcia's for enough cigars and Red Bulls for the round trip, I headed north. I was listening to music when it became crystal clear how I wanted the upcoming book signing back home in Winnetka to go. I called my friend Brad and asked him to open the book signing, with three songs: "Tears in Heaven," "Happy on the Hey Now," and "Old Grief and Love." He would then turn the mic over to Sally. Sally would welcome everyone in her own way and introduce me. It was so clear. I called Brad en route. He had changed plans to make sure he was in town for the event. (My friends are incredible.)

I made it to the empty beach and started walking toward the surf. The white sand was so fine, and the night was beautiful. I walked into the surf and felt something so calming. I felt Chris around me. I first sat and then laid down on the sand. In all my years, I had never seen the stars so beautifully clear and perfectly arranged. Not in Alaska, not in Northern Wisconsin, not in the Caribbean. It was truly breathtaking. My neck was tingling, and I felt Chris close; I thanked him for guiding the book and bringing all the right people into my path. I had texted Sheri Jewel that I was en route to Siesta Key and when I was on the beach, she responded that Chris said I should breathe deeply and look at the stars. Ok I got it. I could just imagine him saying to his pals on the other side, "See, I told you he'd show up."

I was then going to check out the other beach where I felt him, Lido Beach. But I was done in. And I got a message, "Next time Pop." He was letting his tired, old man off the hook. So, I started my trek south to Naples. I am so fortunate and so very grateful for the connection to Chris. For continuing to keep his dad in his life. But this also taught me to trust my gut. Or really, to trust spirit and follow the intuition it has tapped into. If I chose to stay comfortably on the beach in Naples, I would have missed one of the most significant visits with my boy so far in my journey. A mere four hours round-trip to sit on a beach with my Christopher. What parent wouldn't make that trek? Please, listen to your heart.

DECEMBER 10, 2018

Hi Dad. You make me laugh. We did this in a year, and you are already impatient. It's happening. Leave it in my hands. I was content at the Ranch, but happy at the frat house. So, I've got no regrets. Look at the people who I was surrounded by. Still in both of our lives. See, get it? That wouldn't have happened if I stayed on the Ranch. It was my path. Thanks for coming to Siesta Key. I was there but I was also in the car with you driving up there. Hard to understand but it's true. The songs, the call to Brad, it was me. Needed you to wake up so I sent you the dream. And you woke up. I'll take away the bad feelings. Organize your notes & start into Book 2. You will have a following, trust me. Thanks for the kiss, I felt it. I feel your love. Always did. Good meditation music. Yeah, you stumbled on it. Funny. I know you do. I love you too.

Hey Dad, work through the dream. You see me in a suit because I was at a wedding. Of course, I'm not really in a suit. Because that's how you see me. I was at a wedding. I love them here too. We're getting to a new level you and me. Now that the book is published you need to push the envelope and learn more things. You aren't exactly an expert yet. Sorry to tell you ☺. Get the crystal sand from Siesta Key. I will send you the right bottle to hold it. It can be a sign. Like you need one. But I'll send one. Like showing off.

Smiling at you.
Lock it down & come back later.
I love you

What a loving visit from Chris. This is a perfect example of me knowing, absolutely knowing, these messages are from him. In the back of my mind and in my heart, I would always speculate how his life would have turned out if he had stayed at the Ranch, and followed a sober path. But he is quick to tell me, that was my path. He explained that he was happy both at the Ranch and later at the fraternity house. He gently reminded me that if he didn't leave the Ranch, he would have never met the kids at the frat house who provided such a source of love. And he reminded me we would never have met them either. And they are to this day, I mean absolutely to this moment, part of our lives and part of our family.

Chris has come to me in dreams and even once, dressed in a suit. My God, he is a beautiful boy. He lets me know he is running things about the books on his end. I just need to do my part and trust him. That's easy, Chris. The perfect bottle or jars to hold my Siesta Key sand crossed my path as he said they would. Of course, they did.

GALI'S SONG

On December 17, 2018, I was having my first book launch and signing at the Winnetka Community House. We had just published *My Search for Christopher on the Other Side*. When I say "we," I mean myself, my son Chris, and the publisher my boy shanghaied to bring our book into print, Lisa Hagan. The event would be held just a few weeks shy of the third anniversary of the accident.

Here we are three years later at the book signing with a full house of 130-plus people. There were indeed some very special people in attendance. Sally, Caroline, and Will of course. Our in-laws, family, and friends. Our friends, and Chris's friends. High school friends, college friends, these kids who just lovingly won't let go. These are some of the finest people I know. They literally give Sally and me air to breathe with their love and devotion for our boy.

One friend in particular in attendance was Chris's childhood and then young adulthood sweetheart Gali. They began dating in junior high and picked up again when they both ended up in Arizona. Gali was living in Scottsdale and Chris was working at a ranch near Tombstone, while living in Tucson. The Ranch was a therapeutic boarding school and after attending for a year, Chris stayed on as staff. The romance rekindled. Not that it ever really unkindled. I would see Gali when I would come out to spend a long weekend with Chris. We would head up to a resort in Scottsdale and Gali, and later Chris's little brother Will, would join us. Lounging by the pool, spring training baseball games, golf, and steak dinners were the order of the day. It was as close to heaven as I had ever gotten. Their relationship was loving and mature. Gali brought out a tender side in my boy that filled me with pride and love.

As time passed and college loomed, the two drifted apart. Hurt feelings and bruised egos replaced the tenderness and they both moved on. Sally and I were heartbroken as we cared so deeply for Gali, but our children make their choices and so they did.

A year or so after they split, my boy crossed over to the other side and I started my search. It was gratifying and reassuring but it would never compare to a hug, or an "I love you" said in person. You never get over the loss, you just use better tools to cope. Just under three years from his crossing, our dear Gali attended my book signing. Just like she attended the golf outing and concert held in Chris's honor in September. They had a special song… their song, which we covered as a band and dedicated to her. At song's end, there wasn't a dry eye in the house. Including the band members.

The book signing went off without a hitch with the talented Brad Nye performing a few songs including, "Tears in Heaven," by Eric Clapton. I invited a few special mediums to attend and introduced them. One such medium, Andrew Anderson, had become a pal and I noticed him looking at Gali seated in the crowd. At the conclusion of the evening, Andrew approached her and introduced himself. "I don't know you, but you must be someone very special. I know Joe and Chris, and Chris always stands next to or behind his dad during these events. But he stood next to you the entire evening." Andrew and Gali chatted and he did indeed do a reading for her later where Christopher of course came through. Like their youthful relationship, the meeting was magic, and loving, and good. And very much their business. But I do know that Chris will continue to guide and look out for her. You never forget your first love. On either side of the veil.

I had mentioned being with Chris in my dreams. Or I had said that Chris came to me in my dreams. But maybe just maybe

I came to him in my dreams. I had touched on the subject briefly, but maybe we should take a little deeper look at what this all means.

Astral projection or astral travel is an of an out-of-body experience achieved either awake, in a meditative trance, or during a lucid dream state. One must accept the concept that we aren't our body. But rather our body is a physical structure housing our soul. Astral travel is often experienced as the spirit or astral body leaving the physical body to travel in the spirit world or astral plane. I have personally experienced astral travel and visited Chris on the other side. I wake up knowing I have made that journey. I know one can enhance and develop their skills. Which is my plan going forward. Of course, I have not even come close to mastering it. As Chris continues to remind me, I am far from an expert. For a deeper dive into astral projection or astral travel, check out the Appendix at the end of this book.

A CHRISTMAS VISIT

December 23, 2018

I had been feeling low with the holidays in sight. It's tricky. I have two kids who have been crushed by their loss who would like to put all books, interviews, grief, and sorrow away and enjoy their Christmas. They sure deserved it. So, we do what parents do. It's a tricky tightrope really, and if you have or are living through it you know what I mean. We certainly don't practice denial, and it's healthy for kids to know we grieve and love very strongly. But sometimes it's about them. And a Christmas tree and a gift or two or twelve, and love, and even joy can be a part of our life. But unexpectedly, I received my gift early. A really great one.

After visiting and signing books for a neighbor, Cassidy and I jumped into the Jeep and headed over to Sacred Heart Cemetery to visit Chris. I hadn't been there in a few days and so a bit of maintenance was in order. I discarded the two empty Landshark bottles along with a wilted white rose, the remnants of a glass candle, and a withered Christmas corsage. With a damp golf towel, I cleaned the marker and wiped down any stones and momentos left by friends over the last few years. My friend Megan gave me a small cardinal ornament, so I hung it on the little Christmas tree we always place behind the head stone. I sat back in my Bills chair as my dog ran around the cemetery and I smiled, content with my work. I asked my son to send a cardinal, just a gift for his dad.

A man and his daughter were approaching, headed no doubt to a loved one's grave. As the snow always leaves the stones a mess, I offered my ditty bag with cleaning accoutrements, and they went to work on grandpa's stone about fifteen yards away. They returned the bag en route back to the parking lot. The young lady was headed to the local high school next year and they were a hockey family. We knew friends, of friends of friends. After they left, I continued my dialogue with Chris and played his favorite holiday song, "Christmas for Cowboys" out loud on my cell phone. Of course, being who I am, the tears flowed. I hung out a while and then packed up and headed to the Jeep. I loaded everything into the back, including a weary yellow Lab, and started the engine. I plugged in my phone and began listening to a song I had heard for the first time yesterday, "Always Gonna Be You." Then, I lit a cigar while deciding what I would do next.

I had the driver's side door open, and the Jeep was running. I park where I always park, in the circular drive behind the grass island with the big statue of Christ and a huge bush. All of a sudden, a very bright-red cardinal flew across my windshield and landed in the bush not fifteen feet away. He was absolutely luminous and so beautiful. I went to snap a cell phone photo when he nestled deeper into the bush and I heard in my head, "This is just between you and me." I put my phone down and stared lovingly at the bright-red messenger sent by my boy. It was a good five minutes (the song had played completely) and I watched as the cardinal left his perch and headed across the cemetery sky. I sat there in utter amazement. This from a guy who wrote a book about contact with the other side.

As I sit here reflecting on that winter day, Chris gave me a wonderful Christmas present. One that will stay in my heart forever.

CHAPTER TWENTY-THREE:

A McQuillen Christmas

Growing up, Christmas was an amazing time to be a McQuillen. Leading up to the holiday was always very busy. Weeks before, my dad was working round the clock to keep up (or almost keep up) with Mom's Christmas shopping. It was a doubly exciting season because many of the older siblings living out of town always came home for Christmas. It was quasi-mandatory. Christmas always revolved around Clifton Parkway. (The one exception I recall to the mandate was when Billy was in Viet Nam. And we all felt a longing, and a fear. Although he died way too early, he did survive that war and Mom's heart was temporarily healed.) The house was decorated inside and out with Christmas lights. The mantle had a garland and a manger and in front of the fireplace two stone painted Santas stood guard. I believe my sister Debbie still has these. The tree was always big enough to put Chevy Chase to shame. The lights were put on a few days before, but the ornaments could only be applied on Christmas Eve. The icicles were placed on the branches one at a time—which was painful. God forbid if you attempted a shortcut by flinging a few even on the back side of the tree. That exercise would result in best case, stern words, and worst case, an upward slap on the back of the head by one of the older sisters. I suspected they anxiously awaited an opportunity to do that because I was the youngest and a bit of a pill. Sort of a free crack in honor of the birth of the Savior.

Even as a kid, before we moved to the lake, I do have faint memories of Christmas. My belief in Santa Claus was confirmed by hearing sleigh bells and reindeer on the roof in the early morning of Christmas. Years later, I found out our beloved Uncle Bill climbed on the roof with bells and a hammer to pull off the charade. I believe when we did move to the suburbs, that task was assigned to Jerry. To say that we were *all in*—that the McQuillens were all in on Christmas—was an understatement. When we were little, we would come down the stairs to a massive pile of presents. And we would dive in. At first, all the married siblings would bring their babies to the house for Christmas morning. As their babies became children, they all wanted their own Christmas morning at their own homes, and the celebration evolved. At that time, those of us still at home and the single ones who returned home for the celebration all went to midnight mass (at least a part of it) as we habitually arrived late and left early. Meanwhile, Mom and one or two of my sisters were busily finishing wrapping gifts and strategically placing them around the tree. Dad was busy making his baked pepperoni-and-cheese snack, while Bing Crosby crooned on the record player.

When we walked into our home after mass, it was a house transformed into a full-blown Christmas extravaganza. Even though this happened year after year, we were always blown away. Presents were piled all around and halfway up the tree. I remember wondering, Why did they do that? Why all the sixteen-hour shifts, shopping expeditions, and wrapping sessions? I didn't know the answer until much later when I became a dad.

Somewhere in my dad's head, a starter pistol went off and it signaled the beginning of the gift-opening frenzy. I can't remember if we went from oldest to youngest or youngest to oldest, but the frenzy continued on literally for hours. It was amazing. The gifts could range from a pair of pajamas to a bike or a BB gun. But somehow, it always ended evenly. Uncanny, but it did. When the loads of open gifts were strategically placed in piles, we kids would crash, and the wrapping paper would magically disappear and the presents for the morning's festivities would appear. These were for the adult children and their children, plus they would bring their gifts for us, the kids at home. When the morning's events were completed, we would sit down for a wonderful meal of turkey and all that goes with it. There were always two full dining tables, and as a kid, you somehow never got promoted from the kid's table. The week after Christmas each of the married kids had parties at their houses. It was a full week of celebration and love and family.

More than a half century later, I look back on those Christmases long gone by with such fondness and gratitude. Many of those family members have gone home to heaven. I started to name them and then decided to let it be with a single term: family. This will be the fifth Christmas without my boy Christopher. But I take comfort in the knowing (not believing) that he will be with family on Christmas tomorrow. I can still picture him on the steps leading to our living room, our tree obscenely surrounded by presents, waiting to come down and begin the gift-opening frenzy here in Hubbard Woods.

Merry Christmas, Chris… give them all my love xoxo

DECEMBER 24, 2018

Christmas Eve Morning

Hi Pop,

Merry Christmas, I always loved Christmas. I loved being home for it. I'm glad you like my present. I now know you get everything (almost) I send. Listen to the water in the meditation. You are back on the beach with me. Don't worry about the book. I didn't get you this far, I got us this far. I'll handle it. Just do what is in front of you. You don't have to carry the ball Pop. I will. The cardinal on Sunday was so clear. You're on the right path Pop. Time to start writing Book 2 again. Trust the process and trust me. I like the Lily Dale angle. I'll be there. Wait till you see their faces when I'm coming through. I'm pretty powerful and I will be even more so in the summer. See Pop, always summer here. But not really because summer comes to an end. But not here. It's just the way it is. People will ask you lots of questions and I will give you some answers. And some will be, I don't know. That's a fine answer. When you get an idea to send a book remember it comes from me. Just do what you are doing. Time to see a medium or two in July.

Maybe someone new. Think about it. That's always fun for me. Good job Pop I'm really proud of you. I know the closeness can be painful, because of the separation, but that's our deal. That's the way it is and that's the way it's gonna be. It's worth it Pop. It keeps us connected and keeps you in spirit and able to write what I send you.

Merry Christmas Pop. I am Full. Full of love and joy.

The time on the clock isn't a deadline Pop. Just a good time to meet. Thanks for getting up. All the other stuff will work out. You just keep doing what is in front of you. This is your new path Pop. I promise and you will do this work until you come home to me.

Marcia is coming. We are here waiting. She tells you she knows but she will immediately get it. She is loved here and especially missed by Jerry, Pat, & Billy. Her soul family. Me too Pop. Meditate on the Saturday cardinal and know I'm with you all day on Christmas. You always made them special. Love, love, love to Momma. Tell her just that way.

I love you Momma—I'm still your baby boy.
Good job Dad,
Going Back
Chris

Well… that is a precious message. I love that summer never ends where he is. That sounds good to me. Summer and Christopher. Then throw in that the rest of the family is already over there. No wonder I don't fear death. I sure don't need to comment or explain much. He makes himself so clear in this visit. So lovingly clear.

As a parent who lost a child, I want you, the reader, to know I understand the torment and heartache the holidays, especially the big ones, can bring. But it's important to really get our arms around the fact that the ones we are missing so desperately are really in a good place. Take it from a heartbroken dad who has personally heard from, and looked into mediums' eyes as they are communicating with the ones we love and miss. They are good. I mean really, really, good.

And they remember the Christmases, and the birthdays. And they love and recall them with all the love they have in them. And that's A Lot. And that helps. Knowing that, really helps.

CHAPTER TWENTY-FOUR:

LAST VISIT, UNTIL NEXT TIME

JANUARY 3, 2019

You've got a lot to learn Pop. But that's good. We will be together. I will be with you on this journey. So quit worrying. I promise I'm not moving on as I advance. It won't change things with us. Like going up in grades. But you know I'm in the same school. Get it? Clear, right? I told you to be patient about the book. But that's not your style. You crack me up. Don't worry. I'm on it. Three years is your time Pop. Just a day. But I get it. So go ahead, I'll be around. Glad my true pals can come together. I'm there. I'm smiling at you Pop. It's me at my very best. So full of love. Thinking about you and me in the hotel in Tucson. White sheets feeling content. You looking over, and seeing me safe. Me happy, that made you happy. Well, I'm happy all the time now. Know that. Know that as my dad. And we will keep up this journey together. Until you cross over & then I'll bring you across. Actually, you cross over and then I meet you. But you see me and know I'm there the entire time. I'm not sad Pop. Not about anything. We are back together. And that makes me happy. We both are evolving and growing. Thanks for loving my friends. All of them. Look how quickly we connected this morning (morning to you). Opening up Pop. Good job.

The first book was actually about recalling & connecting.
The next one is exploring. I will be your guide & it will be fun.
Find the places. Find the thin places and go there. I'll be there
with you. It will be even bigger than the first book, which will
be pretty big. I wish I could tell the kids how sorry I am about
how I was with them. In time I can. Now, go to bed and think
of watching me in Tucson in the bed next to you. Or lying on the
bed watching the Bills. Or right next to you as a kid. I felt safe
and loved & you did too.

   That's my anniversary gift to you Pop. The safe, loved feeling.
Don't even edit, just go.

Love
Chris

That's the last visit for this book. The story began on January 3
and this book ends on January 3. As is our custom, we all meet
at his grave at 3:30 p.m. and then finish the celebration at our
home. Chris's home. When I started this book, I didn't know
where we would end it. But he did. My Chris did. His visit was so
warm and loving. And so validating. As I write this, I can't help
but cry a bit thinking about those moments on this side when it
was just him and me. Safe, protected, and loved. This visit needs
no other explanation. But that afternoon, his friends came, family
came, and he showed up. If you squint real hard I bet you can
see him in the crowd. Well, maybe not… but everyone sure did
feel him there.

JANUARY 3, 2019

"All stories, if continued far enough, end in death,
and he is no true-story teller who would keep that from you."
~Ernest Hemingway

Well, that's true, and I am in fact a storyteller. But the story is about another place that is right there. Seemingly just out of reach, but it's accessible. You have to do your part. And never, ever lose hope.

As for our family, Sally has gone into private practice as a therapist and her practice is at full capacity. Chris told her it would work out. She is in the final stages of her first book. Like everything she does, it will be amazing. Caroline is finishing up her first year of teaching in Milwaukee, and at semester's end she is going to join her old man in business. How terrific is that? Will is doing well at Boulder. I'm pretty sure this is the summer he cleans his old man's clock in golf. At twenty-one, his looks and mannerisms are so very much like his brother's that it can give one pause. Chris is very proud of those kids. I know… because he has told me.

And me, well my life hasn't changed much since the first book. Last year, at age sixty-three, I hung up my hockey skates. Now, I focus on golf. I have done a slew of interviews and it's been my honor to address groups of parents who have lost kids. Or at least that's how they feel. When not working, I'm usually writing, golfing, or hanging out at the grave at Sacred Heart. It's a good place to visit Chris. If you see me there sometime, swing by and say hello. I'm the guy in the Buffalo Bills chair, smoking a cigar, usually with a Labrador close by. We both miss Chris so much that being there, because we know he's near, somehow takes the pain away. At least for a while.

Hopefully, in a couple of years, we'll be wrapping up Book 3. I know I have work to do on this side. I have grieving parents to reach and a lot to learn. I have a family on this side that still needs me, and I need them. But I want you to know something: I don't need anyone who reads this story to feel sorry for me. I've lived a life beyond my wildest dreams—so much more than I deserved. I married my true love and have amazing children. And I had the greatest job in the world. I got to be Chris's dad on this side for twenty-one years. And I'll continue that role when I join him. And, I'll get to spend the next go 'round with him on the other side. So, when God reaches out and tells me it's time to come home, I'm good. And I mean that. I'm good. They say that heaven is a place where "your dog talks and your father's always young." And I absolutely love that. But with one small addition: it's also the place my Christopher calls home.

I hope this book has given you some comfort, some peace, and some hope.

"And until we meet again. May God hold you in the small of His hand."
~Irish Blessing

EPILOGUE

At age twenty-one, in the early morning hours of January 3, 2016, on chilly Wisconsin Lake Beulah, our son Christopher crossed over to the other side. A year later, I stumbled upon this follow-up article (print version) written by Duaa Eldeib in *The Chicago Tribune*.

Family remains in 'brutal agony' over son's death

Winnetka man, 21, 3 friends died in '16 canoe accident

The McQuillens were eating Christmas dinner two years ago when Chris, the eldest of three children, glanced at his phone and declared he had to go.

He asked his dad to wrap up some roast he could take with him to DeKalb, where he said he'd learned one of his friends at Northern Illinois University was alone on the holiday.

Even as Joe McQuillen fixed the plate and ran to Walgreens for a quick gift for the student, he couldn't help but wonder about his son: "Is he hustling me? Is there a girl waiting? Is there a party I'm missing on Christmas night?"

The next Christmas proved nearly perfect. The McQuillens sat around the fire in their Winnetka home, presents piled beneath their 6-foot Fraser fir. They went bowling, played pool and laughed together.

A few days later, 21-year-old Chris vanished into the night.

He and a group of friends, many home from college on winter break, had met up at a lake house in southern Wisconsin to catch up and celebrate the new year. They watched basketball, ate hot dogs and brats and drank beer, state and police records show.

But around 4 a.m. on Jan. 3, 2016, someone realized that Chris and three others were missing. Several hours later, footprints were discovered in the snow leading to Mill Pond, where a green, three-person canoe lay overturned.

Investigators found a canoe paddle first. Then a winter boot. Inside the house, some of the friends wept. Others stared blankly at each other.

Police, firefighters, neighbors, volunteers and dive teams searched in the icy waters.

One by one, they recovered the bodies of the young men, all from Winnetka or Wilmette: Chris McQuillen, 21; Lanny Patrick Sack, 20; Mori Weinstein, 21. And finally, after five agonizing days, Patrick Wetzel, 21.

Their deaths shook the North Shore community where they lived and had attended New Trier Township High School. Among the four families, the McQuillens agreed to share what their loss has meant to them.

"It doesn't get easier," Joe McQuillen said recently as he sat in a folding lawn chair at his son's grave, a blanket of snow covering the ground. While Chicago Cubs flags dotted the cemetery, the Buffalo Bills keep Chris company. The logo of his dear football team is etched on his headstone and displayed on a golf ball that rests just above his name.

The 'firsts' are the toughest.

Firsts are the most difficult. The first birthday Chris didn't blow out his candles. The first family reunion with Chris absent from the gaggle of cousins. The first Christmas without him. And the first anniversary of his death.

The thought of coming down the stairs this Christmas morning to a house without Chris was too much for his father to bear. So the family exchanged presents a week early, then spent the holiday in Florida.

Maybe next year they'll be able to stay home. For now, it's still about just getting through each day. When they hit emotional land mines, they have learned to find a quiet place and cry. Then they gather up and start again.

"Your grief, in certain ways, the intensity of it is equivalent to the depth of love," said Chris' mother, Sally McQuillen.

A fog initially set in as the family tried to process its loss. People flew in from all corners of the country and even China for the funeral. Sally, a social worker at Evanston Hospital, took a seven-month leave of absence. Family and friends came by the house. For weeks, food showed up on the McQuillens' doorstep.

She said she realized she had to decide if she was going to unravel or push forward. Her two other children, Caroline, 20, and Will, 17, were in pain, as was her husband.

"What I found out is that you can be in the most brutal agony at the same time that you can be in gratitude and joy and love," she said.

As a social worker, she knew how to help others navigate grief, but no amount of practice could prepare her for her own child's death. At work one day, she asked a client if he'd experienced any loss recently, and he mentioned the canoe accident. He had no idea she was the mother of one of the victims.

"It's times like that where I am faced with having to draw upon whatever strength Chris gives me and whatever strength God gives me," she said.

They are all searching for strength.

Joe McQuillen seeks out ways to feel close to his son, even for a moment. He and Caroline organized a golf outing in

Chris' name to raise money for Penguin Players, an offshoot of the Penguin Project, a nonprofit that gives people with disabilities a stage to perform musical theater. As an NIU student, Chris mentored the son of Joe King, Penguin Project coordinator for Children's Community Theatre in DeKalb.

Chris' boundless energy and the way he approached participants as friends, not as people with disabilities, set him apart, King said. "He chose to lead by example in the best way."

Between the golf outing and other donations, $44,000 was raised for a scholarship fund and the Chris McQuillen Spirit Award for most outstanding mentor, King said.

"It's an astounding sum," he said. "I don't know where people find the strength to turn their grief into something so positive, but they did."

Staying busy helped Joe McQuillen and daughter Caroline, a Marquette University junior, deal with the heartache. Joe, a vice president at a Chicago mortgage company, often arrives home exhausted.

"It's not like we're ducking it, but the times you feel (it) are when you stop, when it slows down," he said. "I felt so incredibly close to Chris planning that outing that it was hard when it was over."

At 59, Joe McQuillen is a burly, strong-willed Irishman. His friends describe him as loyal to the end. He acknowledges he was never very neighborly, but he's been overwhelmed by the outpouring of support from those with whom he'd previously only exchanged small talk.

He keeps the lawn chair in his car for his visits to Sacred Heart Catholic Cemetery in Northbrook. He lights a cigar, then he talks to Chris about his day.

How often does he visit his son's grave?

"More than I should," he said. He pauses and begins to sob quietly. "Maybe five times a week."

Sometimes he turns his chair to face the field just behind the cemetery. He remembers the dozens of times he waited for his son to arrive at the airport, his duffel bag slung over his shoulder, and Joe lets himself imagine Chris making his way through the field to come home again.

He takes comfort in his belief that he will hug his son again.

"I'm not going anywhere soon, but most of my life is gone," he said. "I'm rounding third, so that means I'm going to see him sooner than later."

He doesn't ask why they got into the canoe that night. They were kids, he said, good kids who thought it would be a lark to go out on a lake.

Anger would be easier, he imagines. Had Chris been killed by a drunken driver or in war, he would have someone to blame. But Joe has concluded that anger is a wasted emotion.

"Who am I going to be mad at?" he asked. "I'm just sad."

Before his brother died, Will said he had seen his father cry only once, when Casey the family dog died.

"It's like a dagger every time it happens," said Will, a junior at New Trier. His sister places her hand on his arm as he speaks.

Chris was his role model, even if their hobbies did not overlap much. A few weeks ago, when Will couldn't sleep, he got into his brother's Jeep at 3:30 a.m. He blasted country songs, which Chris used to do, and drove to the lake where his brother died. He didn't get out of the car when he arrived, and he didn't gain the closure he was hoping for. But it was what he needed on that day.

'That's what family does'

Chris' godfather, Michael Holmberg, remembers Joe and Sally's joy when their firstborn entered the world in 1994. "They were massively protective," Holmberg recalled. "They were doting and loving and just thrilled." He remembers how it changed Joe. He was a father now, and he was determined to love and hold and cherish his son.

The holding part wasn't always easy. Chris was a pistol from the beginning. By 9 months, he was running. At 2, he wandered into a neighbor's yard to pet their dog.

He was inquisitive, fiercely independent and sometimes defiant. He was also personable and fun, and as he grew up, people gravitated to him. At parties, he was the center of attention without even trying, friends said.

When it came time for high school, his parents enrolled him in military school. After one semester, it was clear that it was not a good fit, and he transferred to New Trier.

Still his parents worried about him, his zeal for adventure and his seeming predisposition for excess. If he was in, he was all in. He had no stop button.

As difficult as it was to see their boy go to a boarding school, after sophomore year Joe and Sally sent him to one in Arizona. He thrived in that slower, structured, sober environment, his parents said. He emerged as a leader and stayed on after graduation to be a mentor and work on a ranch.

But while hiking with a group near the Grand Canyon in 2012, Chris fell down an unmarked mine shaft, his family said.

"We got a call in the middle of the night, and they said they didn't think he was paralyzed, but they weren't sure," his mom said.

Chris was airlifted to the nearest hospital. After months of grueling physical therapy, he recovered. In typical fashion, Chris didn't stop there. He hiked Machu Picchu in Peru.

In 2013, he met his family in Buffalo, N.Y., for the funeral of Joe's niece, who had died of a brain aneurysm. As they were packing to go home, Chris announced he was staying. Someone needed to help take care of her two young sons while their dad coped with his loss.

"That's a hell of a commitment," Joe remembers saying. "That's what family does," Chris responded. He stayed for almost two months.

When people were in need, Chris did not let them down, Sally said.

A lot of Chris — his love of Jimmy Buffett and Hawaiian shirts and the Buffalo Bills — was Joe. The two played golf, went to baseball and hockey games, watched movies together. When Chris' friends came over, Joe would fire up the grill and put on a few steaks.

Along with family, Chris was devoted to his friends. Joe sometimes runs into some of them at the cemetery. On Thanksgiving morning, a group of kids Chris had known since elementary school stopped by the house. Another group of 15 or so friends have asked the McQuillens if they could gather at the house for the Jan. 3 anniversary of his death.

To honor Chris' memory, the world should take a page from his book, Caroline said.

"Be a friend like Chris McQuillen," she said. "Be the guy you can turn to. Be the kind of friend you wish you had."

At NIU, Chris developed especially strong bonds with his Alpha Kappa Lambda fraternity brothers, who still fly a Bills flag in his honor. Mark Cook was the one Chris and a few other friends drove to be with on Christmas night in 2014 when Cook was alone in the fraternity house.

"That was probably one of the happiest moments of my life," Cook said.

At the wake, Cook waited in the long lines that stretched out the door of the funeral home to share that story with Chris' father.

"Mr. McQuillen," he said when he finally made it to the front, "I want to tell you something."

ACKNOWLEDGMENTS

I want to thank my family. For being who they are. They continue to love each other and me though some pretty tough times. I want to thank my friends, who are always, and I mean always there for me. My dog (our dog) Cassidy who is willing to accompany me to the grave to visit Chris. No matter the time. I want to thank Lisa and Lisa for helping me pull a second rabbit out of my hat. I want to thank all the parents who feed my soul with their own stories about their children who, like Chris, stepped across that stream in the woods. And finally, I want to thank my amazing son Chris, for inspiring and loving me, and walking by my side on this extraordinary journey that was chosen for us. I am grateful he will be with me here, until I come home.

ABOUT THE AUTHOR

Joe has been married for thirty years and is the father of three wonderful children—one of whom is now on the other side. Joe was the youngest of ten children from an Irish Catholic family. Although Joe has had two successful careers, he is at heart a blue-collar kid from Buffalo, New York. Joe sits on the board of In Balance Ranch Academy, a boarding school dedicated to helping teen boys with addiction.

Joe is thirty-five years sober and a member of Alcoholics Anonymous (AA), a fact that has helped him get close to God and to carry him through the dark times after Chris's crossing. Not willing to accept a world devoid of his beloved son Christopher, Joe began to research the metaphysical and seek out the answers to that common question, "What happens next?" Joe's book (Joe and Chris's book), *My Search for Christopher on the Other Side*, chronicles the first two years of that journey. Joe assumed that they were "one-and-done" after publishing their first book. But Chris let him know that, in fact, they were not done yet. And so here we are. Joe often speaks to parent groups who have lost kids to the other side. He knows he is being given a gift of connection; a gift that must be given away to keep. He leads his life in two ways: the first is to please his God, and the second is to make his son proud. Following these two tenets makes it hard to go wrong.

APPENDIX

(Or, the place you can find a 'deeper dive' into some of the insightful tidbits and terminology I've shared in this book from outside sources.)

METAPHYSICS

Traditionally, the word Metaphysics comes to us from Ancient Greece, where it was a combination of two words—*Meta*, meaning over and beyond—and *physics*. Thus, the combination means over and beyond physics. In most dictionaries, metaphysics is defined as a branch of philosophy that deals with first cause and the nature of being. It is taught as a branch of philosophy in most academic universities under the label of "Speculative Philosophy," according to the University of Sedona's website.

However, I don't think the study is really beyond the laws of nature. I think our knowledge of the laws of the universe is expanding. Take into account this dialogue from *The Secret*, by Rhonda Byrne:

Speaker: Describe energy.

Scientist: Okay, it can never be created or destroyed; it always was; always has been; everything that ever existed always exists; it's moving into form, through form, and out of form.

Speaker: What created the universe?

Theologian: God.

Speaker: Okay, describe God.

Theologian: Always was and always has been; never can be created or destroyed; all that ever was, always will be, always moving into form, through form, and out of form.

Speaker: You see, it's the same description, just different terminology. You are eternal life; you're source energy; you are God manifested in human form, made to perfection. Scripturally, we could say we that we are the image and likeness of God; we could say we are another way that the universe is becoming conscious of itself; we could say that we are the infinite field of unfolding possibility; all of that would be true.

ASTRAL PROJECTION

A Q&A that may help explain this phenomenon…

By: Jaime Licauco *Philippine Daily Inquirer* / 10:59 PM October 22, 2012

The following are my answers to questions about astral projection asked by De La Salle University student Krysta Mae Alcala for her school newspaper, *Plaridel.*

Q: What is astral projection? What are the scientific and spiritual explanations for this ability?

A: Astral projection or Out-of-Body Experience (OOBE) is not an "ability" or "talent." It is a natural phenomenon or occurrence. It happens to almost anybody, but he or she may not be aware of it.

However, from the point of esoteric science, spirituality and parapsychology, astral projection is a fact. I myself have experienced this many times. But how do we explain the astral body?

Our human constitution consists of several bodies of energy. The astral body is only one of them which is nearest in vibration to the physical body. Usually, the astral body detaches itself during sleep, but sometimes it can also happen while one is fully awake and conscious. The astral body is connected to our physical body through an astral cord or silver cord, which can stretch as far as outer space. There are many reasons the astral body leaves the physical body, such as to give the physical body needed rest, to gain information about the spirit world, to know the future, to meet other astral beings, to heal the sick.

Q: What are the signs that one is undergoing astral projection?

A: This differs from one person to another. To most people, it may appear like they are just dreaming. But when one wakes up during astral projection, he or she may see the physical body lying asleep on the bed while the astral body is on the air near the ceiling. This makes people afraid. But there is no reason to fear. The more a person panics, the more difficult it is to come back. But if one keeps calm, he or she will easily and naturally get back to the physical body.

The astral body is called the "desire body" because it goes where the person subconsciously wants to go. The signs that one is going into astral projection are as follows: He may hear a soft popping sound as the astral body detaches itself from the physical body. Then he may feel the astral wind. His perspective changes, he becomes aware that he is out of the body. If he opens his astral eyes, he sees his physical body asleep on the bed.

Q: *Is this a natural phenomenon or is it inherited? If natural, is there a way to develop this ability?*

A: *It is a natural phenomenon and not inherited as indicated earlier. However, I've met families where several members can go into astral projection at will. Usually, it happens spontaneously without the person consciously doing it.*

NEAR-DEATH EXPERIENCES (NDES)

"The content of a NDE is highly diverse, but commonly include such elements as being out-of-body, seeing others who have died, experiencing peace, unconditional love, a life-review, an intensely beautiful realm and/or all-knowing light or darkness. The experience may also be partly or completely distressing... The NDE is often profound in its message(s) or meaning leading to lasting changes in the experiencer's life. Emotions upon returning from a NDE can be intense, running a range from ecstatic joy to sadness or to anger over being sent back. A long period of integration typically follows a NDE."

Since the term "near-death experience" was coined by Dr. Raymond Moody in his book *Life After Life*, the International Association of Near-Death Experiences (IANDS; www.iands. org), which was subsequently formed to research the experience, collected hundreds of accounts. Twenty-five percent of the reported instances came from people who said they had similar experiences, but were "nowhere near death." The International Association of Near-Death Experiences calls these experiences "near-death-like" or NDLEs.

"Nearing Death Awareness" (NDA) refers to a dying person's experiences in the last few weeks, days, or hours before they die. These may include pre-death or death-bed visions or observations (DBOs) of seeing deceased loved ones or other beings. Additionally, people who were present at a loved one's passing reported that they were briefly taken with their loved one on his or her journey, but were sent back. Others reported feeling the emotions of the dying or dead loved one during their experience. These are called "Empathic Near-Death Experiences" or "Shared-Death Experiences."

A NDE is said to have "veridical" elements if the experiencer—while clinically dead or when conscious thought is supposedly impossible—observed events that were later verified by witnesses. NDEs, reported by young children, instant recoveries from fatal circumstances, sudden development of genius talents or psychic gifts and the experience of sight in the congenitally blind are convincing testimonies that consciousness extends beyond a physical or material existence.

The Forever Family Foundation describes a NDE in this way:

NEAR-DEATH EXPERIENCE

A near-death experience refers to the phenomenon of those who are clinically dead and subsequently revived reporting personal experiences suggesting an afterlife. Although every experience is different, some common themes include detachment and looking down at one's body, presence of a bright light, moving through a tunnel, encounters with deceased people, feelings of warmth and peace, very clear thinking, life reviews, unlimited knowledge, etc. Many are told by various entities to return to the physical world as it is not yet their time to transition. Most experiencers return being absolutely convinced that they visited another realm and therefore lose all fear of death. There are many cases of veridical NDEs, where experiencers report seeing things going on at other's locations such as another room or building. They return with information that can be verified by researchers, such information that they could not have known by ordinary means. Recent developments in cardiac resuscitation techniques have enabled reports of such experiences to increase. There are also near death experience reports from people who were not close to death but faced imminent danger.

NEAR-DEATH AWARENESS (NDA)

The language patients use to communicate NDA may be symbolic and if caretakers are not aware that NDA can occur, patients may be ignored, treated condescendingly, or inappropriately medicated for delirium. Family, friends, and health professionals may respond with annoyance, frustration, or fear. This, in turn, may cause isolation, suffering, and impair the dying person's ability to communicate meaningful experiences at the end of life.

NDA emerges as distinct from delirious states. In general, as opposed to hallucinations in delirious states, NDA occur in clear consciousness; they are reported with clarity, detail, and organization; and they often evoke feelings of comfort, rather than distress.

NDA also differs from deathbed hallucinations with respect to the impact on patients. A study found that NDA tends to be spiritually transformative, while hallucinations tend to be relatively insignificant. In addition, deaths including NDA are more frequently calm and peaceful than are deaths without such experiences. Thus, NDA has been distinctly observed to affect positively the quality of the dying process.

The recognition of NDA requires attentive listening. Health professionals and family, friends can help interpret NDA messages: its content often will vary based on cultural background. Caring for patients experiencing NDA should center on eliciting communication about the experience and accepting their significance for patients and families. Specifically, providers should:

- Evaluate for causes of delirium and treat when appropriate.

- Explore the meaning behind an expression of NDA and its impact on a patient's psychosocial, emotional or spiritual distress. Accept and validate what the patient is telling; do not challenge or argue.

Made in the USA
Columbia, SC
05 July 2022